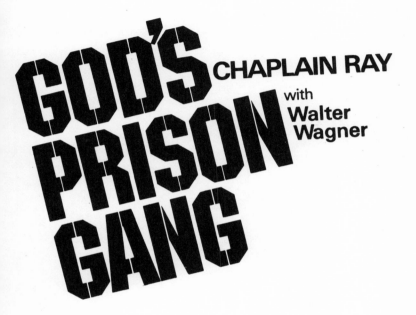

GOD'S PRISON GANG

CHAPLAIN RAY

with Walter Wagner

Fleming H. Revell Company
Old Tappan, New Jersey

Scripture quotations are all from the King James Version of the Bible.

Library of Congress Cataloging in Publication Data

Chaplain Ray, date
    God's prison gang.

    1. Church work with prisoners—United States.
2. Prisoners—United States. 3. Conversion.
I. Wagner, Walter, 1927– joint author. II. Title.
BV4340.C46   253.7′5   76–49571
ISBN 0–8007–0840–7

FOR my wife, Leola, whose untiring
labors have contributed so very much
to this international prison ministry
and whose loving companionship has
made my life a heaven on earth.

Contents

Introduction:

The Long Shadow of Joliet

I was born in 1913, christened Raymond Hoekstra, and in looking back, it almost seems as if I was weaned on the concrete and steel of prison. We lived at the far southern edge of Chicago, not far from the brooding, fearsome walls of Joliet Penitentiary.

As a youngster, I was made very much aware of that escarpment of misery and pain, which was so close to home I could almost fling a stone to the southwest and hit it.

If my two older brothers, John and Herman, or I disobeyed our parents' rules, my father would say, "If you boys aren't good, I'll take you to Joliet." So very early in life we knew that there were places where bad people were taken to be straightened out.

The lessons really hit home, thanks to my Aunt Sarah, who lived in an apartment above us. She would also frighten me into being good with stories about folks in Joliet who'd committed crimes. She spared no details.

Once Aunt Sarah told me about a man who'd killed his wife. Before he was hanged, he was asked if he had any last words. As he stood on the scaffold, waiting to be dropped through the trap door to his death, he said he'd like to sing a song. Aunt Sarah sat down at the piano and sang the condemned man's song in her fine contralto:

> Oh pal, oh gal,
> You have left me all alone.

Oh pal, oh gal,
I'm just a rolling stone.
Shadows that come stealing through the weary night,
Always find me kneeling in the candlelight.
If you can hear my prayer away up there,
Oh pal, why don't you answer me?

I was only seven years old when that incident occurred, but my tender young heart was squeezed by the song. As I grew older, I often thought of that man who'd killed his wife and who at the last moment expressed regret and a soulful prayer for her. I still think of him and the others who were executed in that prison, died in that prison, went insane in that prison, and spent their lives in that prison. Joliet would cast a long, memorable and influential shadow in my life, triggering my initial concern with crime and punishment and their relationship to God and repentance.

But before I could begin my ministry to prisoners, I had to get right with God myself.

My parents had been members of the Dutch Reformed Church. About the time of my birth they became Seventh-day Adventists. As the years passed my father and mother drifted away from the church. I continued to attend for a short period, without, however, having a personal encounter with Jesus.

The family laundry and dry cleaning plant, founded by my grandfather, wasn't making a great deal of money in what was then an area populated by industrious, but poor farmers. Seeking greener pastures, my father moved the family to Berrien Springs, Michigan. The move wasn't a financial success, but though there weren't any luxuries at home, my father did earn enough so that we had food and shelter and perhaps an orange and a few small toys for Christmas.

I skipped a couple of grades in elementary school and was president of the student body in my senior year of high school, class of 1930. That was not a good year for an ambitious young man attempting to get a job. The Great Depression was ravaging America, and there were fifteen million unemployed.

Because my spiritual life was in limbo and I had no godly

direction, I wasn't above lying to obtain work. The job I managed to get was in a furniture factory, doing manual labor. "Blessed are the pure in heart, for they shall see God," says Matthew 5:8. As yet, I had no appreciation of that biblical verity. I only knew that I wanted a job and would lie to get it. But my lie was quickly discovered by a no-nonsense foreman who asked me to produce a birth certificate after I'd been working for a short time. You had to be eighteen to hold a job in the factory, and since I was only seventeen, I didn't have a suitable birth certificate to show him. I quit before he could fire me.

My best friend was a misguided fellow named Ronald Bayles. As the son of a railroad man, he could get a pass allowing him to travel free on any train he wished. He filled my head with romantic tales of the wonders to be found in St. Louis, Kansas City, Omaha, and especially California.

Ronald suggested we head West to seek our fortunes.

"But what happens if we run out of food?" I asked.

"We steal some," he would say.

Joliet flashed into my mind, but I quickly brushed the thought aside.

Ronald's stealing had already resulted in his being a three-time loser. He'd been in two reformatories and one state prison, and he was only eighteen years old. But Ronald was a charming and convincing rascal and I gladly joined him for the trek to California.

The first time I walked the streets of Sacramento, I thought I had reached *Big Rock Candy Mountain.* I saw English walnuts falling from the trees onto the sidewalks and couldn't believe it. Nor could I believe the salubrious climate. But in terms of jobs, the place was sour—there were none.

Ronald and I decided to separate and catch up with each other later. We thought we had a better chance of getting jobs individually rather than together.

I drifted to San Francisco, and one night I was sitting forlornly on the curb of a street, in dire financial need, and with prospects for my future looking as bleak as the dark clouds hovering overhead.

An older man sauntered up to me and said, "Would you like

to make some money?"

"That's what I need alright—money."

"I know a way we can make some. Let's get into my car here and talk."

We walked about twenty feet to a parked Ford, and started to get in. Then a voice said, "What are you doing in my car?"

Thinking fast, my companion told the owner of the vehicle, "Sorry, that's my car right behind you. You can see it looks similar to yours."

I felt sheepish and confused, but I followed the man to the car he'd indicated. His key worked in that one.

As we drove through town, he began talking about money. "I had quite a bit of money the other day, but my partner pulled a gun on me and ran off with it. He left me with only this car."

"How did you get that money?" I wondered about this, feeling downright uncomfortable now.

"We held up young couples who park in lovers' lane in Golden Gate Park. We made quite a bit of money, but now I have to start over again. Why don't you come along with me? You'll make more money than you can spend."

At that moment I turned around and saw a police motorcycle following us. Its red lights were flashing.

"This is a stolen car," the man said. "We better get out of here."

He pushed the accelerator to the floor and away we went, the policeman dogging us. Driving as fast as we could, we zigzagged through the San Francisco financial district, then we got into a hilly area. I knew we couldn't get away, so I said, "When you reach the bottom of the next hill, hit your brake. That policeman behind us can't run in two directions at the same time. You jump from your door and I'll jump from mine."

That's what we did, and it worked. I sprinted like an antelope into a field, making a clean escape. To mask my identity as much as possible, I pulled my coat and cap off, and hid them in a clump of bushes. I rolled up my sleeves and walked along as casually as I could, pretending I lived in the area. I hopped the first street car that came along, reached downtown, got a cheap room, and slept fitfully. I had a nightmare—a black dream in which I was a prisoner at Joliet.

In the morning, I took stock of my situation. I considered myself fortunate to have made my escape. It was even more fortunate that I would never again see my would-be partner in crime.

I hastened out of town as fast as possible and went to Stockton, where luckily I soon found a job as a hired hand on a ranch. I worked there three months. I put a new roof on the rancher's house and I cultivated three hundred acres of land with a sputtering tractor. One of the other hands on the ranch was a Basque from southwestern France. He claimed he was a half brother of Georges Carpentier, who became the light-heavyweight boxing champion of the world by knocking out Battling Levinsky in four rounds in 1920.

I learned to curse handily in the Basque language. But there was a spirit in motion that would shortly cause me to give up cursing and any lingering thoughts I had of doing anything outside the will of God.

After we'd parted, Ronald had hitchhiked to Long Beach, California. He was sitting on a piece of driftwood along the beach one day, wondering where he was going to get his next meal. He was smoking a cigarette. Even today folks seem to be able to get cigarettes, even if they can't get food. Abruptly he became disgusted with smoking. He flipped his cigarette into the tide, and turned and walked into town. Not realizing it, an overwhelming spiritual hunger was gnawing inside Ronald.

By chance, he met a wonderful, ardent Christian lady, who looked kindly at this dark-complected, curly-haired young man who was hungry. She invited him home for supper. Then she told him about Jesus. That night she took Ronald to church and he became a Christian. He spent several weeks going to church every night, enjoying dynamic old-time religion. Then Ronald remembered me, lost as Nebuchadnezzar.

With his few belongings on his back, Ronald hitchhiked to the ranch where I was working. Almost the first words he said were: "I want to tell you about Jesus."

Here was this ungodly, unchurched three-time loser, an ex-convict, traveling three hundred miles to tell a friend who'd been to church as a youngster about God. I knew far more concerning the ways of the Lord than Ronald did—or so I thought. I still wonder at the irony of it and how God uses people in mysterious ways.

Ronald spent the weekend with me, talking non-stop about his new birth and how happy he was. He said he read his Bible all the time, and that Jesus had become the most important force in his life. I couldn't get over it. A short time ago, he was headed for hell. Now his path led straight to heaven.

I watched Ronald very carefully and questioned him closely to see if he was absolutely sincere. He'd been the kind of boy who always liked to tell a risque story; who'd just as soon be dishonest as honest. Yet, I couldn't find a chink in the armor of Christ that Ronald was wearing. He'd lost all interest in risque stories and thoughts of crime. His only interests were Jesus and the Bible.

That glorious weekend with Ronald influenced me tremendously. I decided that I wanted to come to God, too. But how? I didn't even own a Bible.

In the bunkhouse I found an old song book with the words to "Lord, I'm Coming Home."

That inspired William J. Kirkpatrick hymn had a profound effect on me as I sang a cappella:

> I've wandered far away from God,
> Now I'm coming home;
> The paths of sin too long I've trod,
> Lord, I'm coming home.

Tears gushed like rivulets from my eyes. That song was written for me—the prodigal who wanted to come home. Still, I didn't know my way home. I was prepared for the journey, but had no transportation.

The job at the ranch ended at the same time that I began

to yearn for Jesus. I packed, which wasn't a difficult task. Everything I owned was in a string-tied bundle that I carried on my shoulder.

I went to San Jose, where I'd heard there might be jobs. But before looking for work, I looked for a church. The first church I found that had its door open was the Anchor Rescue Mission. I went in and sat down in the last pew.

A missionary, newly returned from Africa, was speaking. I can't remember one word of what he said, but I can still see him in my memory, gesticulating with enthusiasm and, I'm sure, calling for the Word to be spread to every living creature throughout the world.

When the sermon ended, the choir sang an invitation. It just so happened their song was "Lord, I'm Coming Home." I found myself singing along:

> I've wasted many precious years,
> Now I'm coming home;
> I now repent with bitter tears,
> Lord, I'm coming home.

When the hymn concluded, I had an overwhelming desire to go directly to the altar. But I couldn't move. I held on to the bench in front of me with both hands. My knuckles turned white. I stood there, frozen. An older Christian lady who obviously knew a good deal about the workings of the Holy Spirit came walking down the aisle. She saw the look on my face, and saw how moved I was. She saw my hands gripping the seat. Tenderly, she reached over and laid her hands on mine. "My son," she said, "the Lord wants you to come tonight—now."

My hands relaxed and a moment later I was at the altar, kneeling and praying. Again the rivulets of tears came, so many that there was a veritable puddle.

The lady who'd urged me forward was behind me. I heard her say, "Thank God for *real* repentance." Evidently they'd seen a good deal of the other kind.

I spent that evening in a room at the mission. I never slept so soundly and so peacefully as on the night that Jesus enveloped me.

The morning after I gave my life to God, I found a miracle had occurred. God had created a new heaven and a new earth for me. Everything was different than I had known it the day before. Never had I been as happy, as content, and as serene. It wasn't "Lord, I'm Coming Home," it was "Lord, I *Am* Home."

I spent a week at the mission, studying the Bible and attending prayer meetings. Those enthusiastic evangelical encounters were *manna* for my soul. I thrived on the experience. I've been thriving ever since. Never—not once—have I looked back in doubt or regret.

Next, I began a period of intensive Christian study which led to my ordination. The Lord blessed me mightily. Only four years after my conversion, I became the pastor of Calvary Church, a small independent house of God in Indianapolis, Indiana. It had only thirty-two souls at the time, but an avid drive for new members and perhaps my own fervor resulted in a vastly increased congregation. The church became a strong vessel for God.

I was invited to preach at a church in New York, and after my message, a member of the congregation asked me if I wanted to visit Sing Sing, the Hudson River prison, which, next to Alcatraz, had the most foreboding reputation of any institution in America. The congregation member who'd asked me had a friend who worked there, Officer Malcolm Taylor.

He met me at the gate and gave me a complete tour of the prison where many of the most dangerous criminals in the nation were incarcerated. Our last stop was the Death House. Officer Taylor, who'd spent many years on Death House detail, had me sit in the electric chair. I made certain that the heavy copper wires that carried the current to the chair were disconnected before sitting in the seat where hundreds of prisoners had died.

"Sometimes we have mass executions here," Officer Taylor said. "I've seen as many as seven die in one night."

I asked: "In all the years you've served on the Death House squad, seeing so many die, what percentage of those about to go to their deaths sought spiritual comfort, asked Christian help, or requested a minister or a priest?"

Officer Taylor said: "It would be hard for me to recall a single prisoner, even the toughest of them, who didn't."

This visit to Sing Sing reinforced my belief that the Lord was calling me to a special ministry for prisoners.

From my Indianapolis church, I'd already made frequent visits to the Indiana reformatory at Plainfield and the state prison at Michigan City. I'd served as sponsor for a number of young prisoners. After their release I would help them get jobs and counsel them in the ways of the Lord. If any of them who became born-again Christians ever returned to prison, I never heard about it.

Since those first visits to prisons, I've devoted my life to aiding prisoners through Jesus. Hardly a week passes before I visit one or more of the three hundred prisons in America.

I make it a practice to seek out some of the most notorious criminals in the country who've had conversion experiences. They tell their stories to me, which I then print in my literature and broadcast on my radio programs. Nothing impresses our current inmate population more than these absorbing tales of ex-cons made whole again through Christ.

The years of my prison ministry have been ripe and rewarding—but there remains so much to do, so many souls to be won. I've never kept count of how many prisoners I've helped lead to the Lord, or of how many prisoners my visits, literature and broadcasts have aided. Still, from the thousands of letters of appreciation I receive each year, I know the number has been large.

Today my headquarters is in Dallas, Texas, one of America's ten largest cities. It's been said that there are more Bible-carrying Christians and churchgoers in Dallas than in any other city in America, a distinction that makes *Big D* proud. Dear to our hearts are two Dallas churches, the First Baptist Church, which has 19,000 members and is pastored magnificently by Dr. W.A. Criswell, and Calvary Bible Church, whose gifted pastor is my son, Robert Lee Hoekstra, a graduate of Dallas Theological Seminary.

Whatever happened to Ronald Bayles who was so instrumental in my coming to Jesus? Did he lose his faith and go back to prison, or did he cleave to Christ?

I still see Ronald frequently and recently he told me, "You know, once I could do a one-to-ten-year prison sentence standing on my left ear in the corner of my cell. Prison didn't intimidate me. I didn't give up crime and that life because I was afraid of prison. I did it because I met Jesus."

Ronald became a minister! Now retired, his last pastorate was at the Assembly of God Church of Torrance, California, which he served for thirteen years. His daughter, married to a fine Christian, is a missionary in Africa.

As for me, the long shadow of Joliet has been gone since the night I was saved. I've been back to Joliet a number of times, but only as a visitor, to minister in the prison chapel and share with others what I received that night in San Jose, California —the grace of Christ which has led me down the fulfilling road of Christian service.

1

The Conversion of Susan Atkins

What I consider the crime of the century began on a humid Friday night in August 1969.

The moon was an aureole of white heat as four stealthy figures, clad in black, approached the rented Sharon Tate mansion in Bel Air, California. High on drugs and bent on murder were Charles (Tex) Watson, Susan Atkins, Patricia Krenwinkel, and Linda Kasabian.

Mrs. Kasabian, divorced from her first husband and estranged from her second, was posted as lookout while the three other intruders entered the Cielo Drive home after midnight.

When they departed, their spoor was a human slaughterhouse—the unprecedentedly savage killing of five people, a crime so vile, ignoble and horrible that even now it still has the capacity to shock, outrage and bewilder the God fearing. How could our Judeo-Christian society produce such young, vicious killers?

Lying dead in the splendidly appointed house were movie star Sharon Tate; Jay Sebring, an extremely successful men's hair stylist; Voityck Frykowski, an aspiring film writer and assistant director; coffee heiress Abigail Folger; and Steven Parent, an eighteen-year-old acquaintance of the caretaker on the estate.

One by one the five had been brutally butchered. Frykowski alone was shot twice, hit at least thirteen times on the head with a blunt instrument, and stabbed no less than fifty-one times. Miss Tate, who was eight months pregnant, had pled frantically for the life of her unborn child. To the "music" of her pleas, as Susan Atkins later described it, she, too, was stabbed repeatedly, in her neck, breasts, and back. The murders were discovered later that Saturday morning.

The following day, Sunday, in another part of Los Angeles, the murderous quartet was joined by Leslie Van Houten to kill, with equal ferocity, Leno and Rosemary LaBianca. Mr. La-Bianca, who ran a chain of supermarkets, was found with a bloodstained pillowcase over his head. There was a lamp cord around his neck. A leather thong had been used to tie his hands. A carving fork protruded from his stomach. There were myriad stab wounds in his abdomen. The word WAR had been carved on his naked flesh.

There were so many stab wounds in the body of Mrs. La-Bianca that at first investigators didn't even try to count them. Like her husband, her head was shrouded by a bloody pillow-case with a lamp cord wound around her neck.

Before leaving the LaBianca residence, the murderers, using the blood of the tragic couple, scrawled six words on the walls of the house, DEATH TO PIGS; RISE; and HEALTER SKELTER (mis-spelled).

The crime triggered the most intensive police hunt in Los Angeles history. The trail led at last to the semidesert Spahn movie ranch, the home of a Family of hippies, led by the fire-eyed Charles Manson. Investigators learned that Manson had not only ordered the seven killings, but had committed the ultimate blasphemy—he convinced his followers he was "Jesus Christ." Members of the Family often called Manson "God" or "Jesus." Jesus Himself anticipated such false prophets as Charles Manson in Mark 13:6: "For many shall come in my name, saying, I am Christ; and shall deceive many." Neverthe-less, it was unbelievable that the bright shining Son of God who had walked Galilee's shores and preached peace, humility, gentleness, kindness, and nonviolence, had had His name usurped by Manson, a lethal drug addict bearing the mark of Cain.

A nine-and-a-half-month murder trial ensued for Manson and his principal female acolytes. Linda Kasabian became a witness for the prosecution.

In the courtroom, the three girls were a study in remorseless villainy. Their eyes, particularly those of Susan Atkins, came alive only when they rested on Manson, who glowered, cursed, and blamed everyone but himself for the bloodletting he had instigated.

The backgrounds of the girls belied their involvement with Manson and mass murder.

Patricia Krenwinkel, whose parents were divorced, had briefly attended a small Catholic college, Spring Hill, in Mobile, Alabama, before she joined the Manson Family. Despite that training, she'd never come to know Jesus as her personal Savior. When she met Charles Manson in Los Angeles, she instantly quit her job, not even bothering to pick up her paycheck. She also left her car abandoned in the parking lot. Later she wrote her father a cryptic note, saying, "I'm trying to find myself."

Leslie Van Houten's father was a Monrovia, California, auctioneer and her mother a schoolteacher. Growing up, she was considered an all-American girl. She sang in the youth choir at the Village Presbyterian Church and attended Sunday school faithfully. But Miss Van Houten, too, had failed to accept Jesus as the spiritual guide for her life. After her parents divorced, she drifted far from middle-class life, taking up with Manson and becoming one of his most devoted harem girls at the Spahn ranch, located about forty miles from Los Angeles.

The background of Susan Atkins was the most punishing. Her father went bankrupt in the construction business in San Jose, California, and her mother died while she was in high school. Both her parents became alcoholics. Susan quit school in the eleventh grade at the age of eighteen. She ran away from home when her father attempted to molest her. As a youngster in Sunday school, she'd been an *A* student. On one occasion she was rewarded with a white Bible for her diligent scholarship. After the death of her mother, her attitude toward religion changed. "I had no visible proof that there was a God," she said. She accused the members of her church, her minister, and the deacons of hypocrisy—"None of them believed in the

Bible." Needless to say, she had also rejected Christ. Susan had lived a promiscuous life as a topless dancer in Los Angeles and San Francisco. Then she ran into Manson and the cult leader hypnotized and "converted" her as he had the other members of the Family.

Sitting at the defense table, Susan Atkins, a slim attractive brunette in a pink velvet dress, stared daggers into Linda Kasabian as she gave her sensational and damning testimony.

According to Mrs. Kasabian, Tex Watson had killed Voityck Frykowski. She saw Watson confronting him with an upraised knife. Before plunging the blade into his body, Watson screamed: "I'm the devil. I'm here to do the devil's work."

Mrs. Kasabian implicated all four defendants. As an eyewitness her testimony was irrefutable.

The picture that emerged during the trial was that Charles Manson had a grudge against society. He was violently envious of anyone who was successful and wealthy. He'd drawn up a "hate list" and planned to order the execution of six celebrities. All were to be killed with unthinkable, virtually unprintable torture. Frank Sinatra was to be skinned alive; Steve McQueen, boiled in oil; Doris Day, raped and impaled; singer Tom Jones was to have his tongue ripped out; Elizabeth Taylor would have her breasts cut off; and Richard Burton was to be castrated.

Eighty-four witnesses and some three hundred exhibits were introduced at the trial. At one point in the procedure, Manson, obviously alluding to Christ, testified: "I've been dead two thousand years." The judge cut off prosecutor Vincent Bugliosi when he attempted clarification and elaboration of the remark.

Summing up, Bugliosi said that Manson's messianic ravings were not about love but about hate, violence, lust, sexual depravity, and ritual murder. Manson saw himself as a kind of messiah, a messiah, who, just as in the Bible, was the creator of a new way of life. The poor and the dispossessed—particularly young girls—were offered a place at the Spahn ranch where they could feel accepted. But the price for this *paradise* was sex, drugs, and murder. Manson, Bugliosi told the jury, was hardly Jesus Christ.

Though Manson had not personally been present at the

killings he was nonetheless "as guilty as sin," Bugliosi said. Like some demoniac general, Manson had sent out his troops to kill the *pigs,* the *enemies.* Manson had fantasized a war between blacks and whites. The lyrics of a Beatles' song, "Helter Skelter," had somehow been misinterpreted by Manson to signify the outbreak of hostilities between the races. Manson, Bugliosi concluded, was "one of the most evil, satanic men who ever walked the face of the earth."

The jury agreed. The four defendants were found guilty. Tex Watson was later tried separately. All five received the death penalty. Their sentences were commuted to life imprisonment after the Supreme Court outlawed capital punishment.

The shattering case was closed and like the rest of civilized mankind, I put Manson and his colony of murderers out of mind, although now I made it a habit to double-check the locks on the doors of my own home.

I thought perhaps one day I would possibly be in contact with Manson and/or his followers. In the four decades of my prison ministry, I had already crossed paths with some of the most notorious criminals in American history. But I did not seek out Manson or any member of his Family, feeling that their crimes were so heinous, their minds so warped, that it would undoubtedly be useless to attempt to talk to them about the things of God. I felt the Lord would lead me to the Manson clan at the right moment.

Meantime, I continued my work, sending Bibles and other Scripture material to prisons, visiting prisons, publishing my magazine, *Prison Evangelism,* and broadcasting my daily *Cellblock* program over the Mutual Broadcasting System plus additional broadcasts on more than one hundred independent radio stations.

The monstrous Manson case didn't come to my attention again until almost five years later, when I received what is perhaps the most remarkable and unexpected letter I've ever read. Dated December 31, 1974, it was addressed to me in Dallas.

"Greetings in Christ's name to you and your blessed ministry," the letter began. "I'm an inmate in the California Institution for Women and am presently housed in what was the Death Row. My death sentence was commuted to life in 1973, by law. In 1974, my life sentence was commuted to eternal life in Christ. Praise the Lord that He would touch even me and restoreth my soul."

Curious, I turned to the signature on the three-page letter, written on flower-bordered stationery. I gasped when I read the name: Susan Atkins! The Lord had provided the right moment! I hurried on to read and exult in the rest of the letter.

"This is the first time I've written you," Susan Atkins said. Her penmanship was firm and mature. "It's only after listening to many of your radio programs and hearing the testimonies of many blessed and beloved brothers in Christ behind prison walls all over this country that I felt a nudging to write you.

"I've been isolated from the main-line population since my incarceration here at C.I.W. and been unable to attend any church service and Bible study classes because of political situations concerning my case and name, but praise God and His beloved Son, for He touched even me when I had no way of reaching out to a congregation in fellowship."

Miss Atkins continued, "It is my prayer, that through your ministry He will touch many more men and women inside prison so that they who are able to would seek Bible study classes and go to the church services at whatever prison they are in, and seek fellowship with their fellow brothers and sisters inside and outside."

"Jesus Christ," she concluded, "is my dearest friend as I serve my life sentence. Chaplain Ray, I'm not exactly sure why I'm writing you all this, but I'm assured He knows why and will rest assured that my small testimony to you will be of benefit and an inspiration to you."

A jumble of thoughts cascaded through my mind. Should I take the letter at face value? Should I believe that the conversion of Susan Atkins was real? Had evil transmuted itself into good? After all, she was not a complete stranger to God. She'd attended church as a child and had often heard Manson misuse the name of Christ. Then I thought, Was Susan Atkins professing Christianity solely to win sympathy and privileges from prison authorities and a possible parole? In my long years of dealing with prisoners, I had become well aware of the phenomenon known as "jailhouse religion"—a cynical device characterized by an insincere conversion, used by some prisoners to curry favor with guards, wardens and the parole board. But what if Susan Atkins had truly come to Jesus? What right had I to doubt? Still, I had to find out for myself.

Susan Atkins, Patricia Krenwinkel, and Leslie Van Houten were imprisoned in a specially constructed unit at the California Institution for Women at Frontera, near Los Angeles.

Their world consisted of three small cells, an adjoining study room, and a high, durably fenced recreation yard which offered a view of snowcapped mountains to the north and the smog of Los Angeles to the west.

The three young women were closely guarded twenty-four hours a day. They had their own matron and supervisor. They were totally isolated, except from each other. (They have since been transferred to a larger unit, with forty other women prisoners.)

The expression on Susan Atkins' face was buoyant and radiant, as distant as possible from the sullen, abrasive countenance of the Manson puppet who'd stood trial and been sentenced to death.

She welcomed me effusively, saying, "Praise the Lord. I never thought I'd meet you. I never thought you'd come to see me."

Susan introduced me to Patricia Krenwinkel and Leslie Van Houten. They seemed subdued and resigned to their fate. I would have talked to them about Jesus, but there wasn't time. My pass was for the express purpose of visiting with Susan.

We sat on comfortable chairs in a small room about eight feet square in a vestibule off the main entrance of the quarantined unit, a guard listening to everything we said.

My first question to Susan was, "How did you become a Christian?"

"I started by reading the Bible and then I began listening to your broadcasts. Also, I had a letter from Bruce Davis, saying he was a Christian."

Davis was a second-level member of the Manson Family,

who is serving a life sentence for his participation in the Manson-ordered slayings of music teacher Gary Hinman and ranch hand Donald Jerome (Shorty) Shea. Davis was the first member of the Manson Family to become a Christian, and his decision for Christ had impressed Susan.

"I thought if Bruce could walk with the Lord, so could I. If God could forgive Bruce, I thought He might forgive me."

"Susan," I said, "you can't embrace the Lord *and* Charles Manson."

She ran her hand through her hair, pursed her lips and replied in a soft, sure voice: "I've cut all my ties to Charlie. I no longer consider myself a member of his Family. I'm now a member of the family of God."

Susan said she wasn't bitter or antagonistic toward Manson. "I pray for him. I pray that Charlie and all the other members of the Family will turn to Christ, and turn away from the life-style that led them to commit murder. You know, Chaplain Ray, there's even hope that Charlie may come to the Lord one day."

Perhaps Susan's optimism is justified. Manson, before he was transferred to Folsom Prison from San Quentin, asked for a Bible. My friend, Chaplain Harry Howard, who dealt with Manson at San Quentin, says cautiously that Manson appears open to the Christian faith, though he has not undergone a conversion. Adds Chaplain Howard: "Manson told me, 'Everybody must come to the Cross—either voluntarily or they will be dragged to the Cross in judgment.' "

Having ignited the crime of the century, it could be said that Charles Manson's embracing the Lord would be the conversion of the century.

Full of faith, Susan preferred to dwell less on Manson than on the miracle of how she received Christ.

"One night, as I was lying in bed in my cell, I found myself thanking God. I thought, *What am I thanking Him for?* The answer came swiftly, *For the peace and joy I suddenly felt.*

"I got off the bed and down on my knees to pray."

"The presence of the Lord came into my little cell like liquid waves of glory. It swept my whole being. God was so real and so close that I was enveloped in Him.

"I found myself worshipping the Lord and praying to him in words I had never before known or uttered.

"Since that visitation from God, I feel His presence always. My cell has been transformed into a temple of worship. I no longer feel like a prisoner. I feel like a servant of the Lord.

"Chaplain Ray," Susan said, "since God saved me from the death sentence and Death Row, and changed my sentence to eternal life with Him, I have so much to be thankful for. Here I have a lot of time to read the Bible, to study, and to correspond with Christian friends. I'm so grateful for the blessings I've received."

Still speaking with animation, Susan said she planned to be baptized. And she was, shortly after my visit. The ceremony, symbolizing union with Christ, was performed by Reverend Sarge Wright, who'd known Susan in her childhood. A handful of witnesses, standing near a metal tank on the front lawn of the prison chapel, looked on as Reverend Wright asked Susan, "Daughter, do you know that this means your sins are forgiven by Jesus—everything you've ever done?"

"Yes," she replied, and then she was immersed.

The time for our visit was drawing to a close. As we came to the end of our talk, a luminescent quality suffused Susan's features. Her complexion, once mottled by the aftereffects of drugs, was now clear. She was all smiles, earnestness and candor.

I had no doubt that she had come to Jesus. I felt as comfortable with Susan as I would in church. It seemed apparent that the lance of Christ had given her a protective weapon against prison and the enmity of millions of Christians who still thought of her as a child of the devil.

Now Susan turned her hands palms upward and said, much to my surprise: "I thank God that these two hands of mine have never taken a human life."

I gazed mutely at Susan Atkins. Every account I had read of the Tate-LaBianca slayings had implicated her. Now she was claiming she was innocent of murder by her own hand.

As I walked back to my car, my head swam. Again, I felt impelled to discover the truth. There was only one man in the world who could confirm or deny Susan Atkins' statement, and I was going to visit him the next day.

2

"A Human Vegetable"

The letter from Tex Watson's mother said: "You would have had to know Charles to know what kind of boy he was before Manson got hold of him. He was a typical young American boy. He still holds the record in school for the high hurdles. He was a star at football, basketball, and track. Our prayer now is for him to be a star for Jesus, to help young people not to follow the wrong leaders and involve themselves in drugs."

The outspoken Mrs. Watson also wrote: "We saw Bugliosi on TV, trying to sell his book, *Helter Skelter*. He took the transcripts of the trials and wrote this book. No one really knows what happened in the Manson murders, except what the young people told at the trials. They were all so drugged I can't see how they could remember if they murdered anyone, and how they could live with themselves if they did.

"I don't believe Bugliosi when he says Charles will be in prison for fifteen or twenty years. I pray so many times a day for God to touch Charles in a very special way. I know He will.

"Please do anything God would have you do for Charles."

Mrs. Watson's letter arrived at virtually the same time as that of Susan Atkins. So in addition to scheduling a visit to Susan, I arranged with Chaplain Stanley McGuire, the inmate shepherd at the California Men's Colony at San Luis Obispo, to see Tex Watson on the same trip.

Of all the strange facets of the Manson case, perhaps the strangest is the 180-degree turnabout in the character of Tex Watson.

The youngest of three children, he grew up in Copeville, Texas, a microdot community with a population of 150. His parents are stable and hard working. For twenty-nine years, they've run a small service station and general store twenty-five miles northeast of Dallas. The family is law-abiding; a cousin is a county sheriff.

Tex Watson was a model student. He never made a grade below *B* in high school. In addition to his athletic ability, he was sports editor of the school yearbook. By the time he enrolled at North Texas State University, he was a tall, handsome and ambitious youngster majoring in business management. After three years in college, he inexplicably dropped out, moved to Los Angeles, and in 1967, joined the Manson Family.

A friend in Los Angeles remembers him before and after: "This nice guy who came out here from Texas had become someone else. He was a completely different personality. He was almost incoherent at times. He had very little communication with anyone he had previously known in the straight world."

During his trial, Tex had been imprisoned in county jail. After his conviction, he was sent to San Quentin's Death Row. When his sentence was commuted to life, he was moved to an ordinary cell and allowed to mingle with other prisoners. Then the administration learned there was a contract on Tex's life, that he was marked for murder. He was transferred to C.M.C, a maximum security institution that allows inmates many privileges. Each prisoner has his own cell, which does much to eliminate inmate violence, homosexuality, strikes, riots, frustration, resentment and anger—problems all too common in most U.S. prisons. Tex is among those prisoners who are allowed to carry the keys to their own cells. They can lock themselves in, and they can lock the cell when they leave. The grounds are beautiful and park-like, the administration is wise and enlightened, and runs a fine facility.

Understandably, C.M.C. is a favorite of prisoners, who would rather serve their sentences there than in the tougher California penitentiaries, San Quentin, Folsom and Soledad. At the latter an average of at least one inmate a month is killed by fellow prisoners.

Chaplain McGuire met me at the front gate and escorted me to his office, which adjoins a large, lovely interfaith chapel. Waiting for me was a tall, young man with deeply set eyes and dark hair, who appeared to be somewhat shy. He rose when I entered. Chaplain McGuire said to me, "This is Tex Watson."

We shook hands. Tex Watson's grip was soft and tentative. His manner was unassuming and contrite. He was clean-cut and alert, his eyes brimming alertly. He could again have been that North Texas State college student. He was anything but "a human vegetable," which a reporter had dubbed him at his trial.

Tex wasn't a committed Christian. He was not an unbeliever or a disbeliever. He was a young man who had grown up attending a small Methodist country church with his family without ever making a personal commitment to Christ. How different his life would have been and the lives of so many others if he had made that commitment.

Chaplain McGuire had told me that Tex had been some-what withdrawn, refusing to converse, except when necessary, with other inmates and the staff. But, for whatever reason, he had no hesitation in talking to me. He revealed a good many heretofore unpublished details about the Tate-LaBianca killings and his life with the Manson Family.

Tex said that while he was in county jail, other members of the Family, who were in the same cellblock, had attempted to communicate with him. But, he said, he'd already broken emotionally with them and withdrawn his loyalty to Manson.

I told Tex about God's attitude toward prisoners and what the Bible has to say about prisons and prisoners. I told him that Jesus was a prisoner and numbered among the transgressors. I recounted my visit to the old quarter of Jerusalem where I had seen the ancient prison cells that date back to the time of Christ. I said I had visited the place where Jesus was said to have been imprisoned after He was arrested in the Garden of Gethsemane.

"In our society most folks are very careful with whom they associate," I said. "We try only to associate with people who can advance our careers and benefit us financially. But Jesus identified with the poor, the rejected, with the sick, with the afflicted of mind and body, with criminals, the dispossessed, and with the disenfranchised. And, Jesus was crucified between two thieves."

Tex seemed extremely interested in what I was saying. And he was familiar with the Bible. He said he'd done quite a bit of Bible reading in jail and on Death Row. It began as an alternative to prison madness. Then, at C.M.C. he got deeply interested in Scripture, absorbed the Book voraciously, and began to seek God's help for his troubles. He still hadn't put his hand in the hand of the Lord, but he'd made a beginning by asking the Lord to give him aid and comfort.

"Susan Atkins," I said, "would like to share with you the good news of her conversion, how she's become a happy Christian and has found peace and forgiveness and a new life in Christ. Susan feels strongly attracted to you, Tex, and has very fond feelings for you."

"It's true that there was a special feeling between Susan and me when we were members of Charlie's Family," Tex said. "We used to keep some drugs hidden, and when we had a chance, we'd do drugs together—*LSD* and other things. In fact we did some drugs together just a few hours before the killings."

"Susan also said that the women in the Manson Family were trained to take a secondary position and that their lives were not as important as those of the men. She told me that the girls involved in the killings were willing to do everything possible to protect Manson and you, even to the extent of confessing to the crimes and absolving Manson and yourself," I continued.

"That's true," Tex Watson affirmed. Suddenly tears began streaming down his face. "Those killings," he said, "were so terrible. I find it hard to forgive myself, taking all those lives. When I remember all those poor people we put to death, I wish there was something that I could do to make it right."

"If it were possible," I asked, "would you be willing to give your own life to bring those victims back from the grave?"

"Yes!" he said instantly. "I only wish I had that chance."

There was a long pause while Tex dried his tears.

I then remembered one of the reasons for my visit. "The last thing Susan Atkins said to me," I told Tex, "was that her hands had never taken a human life. You were there when the people at the Tate mansion were killed. You were there when the LaBiancas were murdered. Only you can tell me if Susan is telling the truth."

"She's telling the truth," Tex Watson said. "She didn't kill anyone. I killed them all!"

Tex added an extra shock. "On Manson's orders, I was present and involved when Shorty Shea was killed." Shea had been associated with the Family, Tex said, but Manson didn't trust him. "That's why Charlie wanted him dead. Charlie and some of the others in the Family finished the job of killing Shorty. His body was chopped up and buried there on the ranch."

Tex said that Manson's hold on him was complete, and he only murdered on Manson's orders. After killing everyone in the Tate home, Tex said he and the others left the scene in a little Ford. They went up a canyon road and saw a house with a garden hose in front. They stepped out of their car to wash the blood off their hands. The owner of the house came out and asked what they were doing. He ordered them off the property, saying if they didn't leave at once he'd call the police. Tex and the others ran. He had just killed five people, but he ran nevertheless. He could easily have killed that man, but he didn't harm a hair on his head because Manson hadn't ordered that slaying.

Tex said that when they entered the Sharon Tate house, they didn't know who was going to be present. Manson had ordered them to kill everyone at the Terry Melcher home. Melcher, who is Doris Day's son, was no longer living there. Manson hated Melcher because he refused to finance the recording of Charlie's wild, rambling, and *crazy* songs.

Tex declared that the LaBiancas had been chosen for murder virtually at random. Tex told how he, Manson, and the girls had driven around for hours looking for a likely victim, because Manson wanted someone, anyone, killed. They finally stopped at the LaBianca residence. They chose that house because they knew it; they'd had a drug party in the empty house next door a few months before.

They quickly overpowered the LaBiancas. Manson had a couple of leather thongs hanging around his neck, which he and Tex used to tie the LaBiancas' hands. Manson ordered Susan Atkins to accompany him back to the ranch. Then he commanded Tex and the other girls to kill the helpless couple.

With those chilling, startling admissions, my first visit with Tex Watson was concluded. It remained only for us to pray. I called on God to bless Tex with the same miracle of deliverance He had performed for Susan Atkins, and I also asked God to bring all the other members of the Manson brood, including Manson, to His throne.

My initial confrontation with Tex had accomplished much. It got him talking. It overcame his reticence. It resulted in his telling openly, for the first time, his role in eight killings. Our conversation had also lessened his profound feelings of guilt.

Tex was an excellent example of many prisoners who become so penitent about their crimes that they can't forgive themselves for what they've done. That often keeps them from accepting Christ. So in subsequent visits and in letters I constantly reassured Tex of Jesus' promise not to cast out anyone. I reminded him repeatedly that there is no crime that any man can commit that is beyond the reach of God's mercy and forgiveness.

Tex began attending the prison chapel, and giving his testimony. Now, when he talked about his past, he no longer wept. I had underlined in his Bible in 2 Corinthians 5:17, "Therefore if any man be in Christ, he is a new creature: old things are passed away; behold, all things are become new."

After Tex gave his life to Christ, he was allowed to leave his job as an aide to the prison psychiatrist in order to work in the chapel. Tex has become so fervent a Christian that he is now a deacon in the prison church and song leader at the services I hold whenever I visit C.M.C. Tex is also studying for the ministry, and he has the confidence of the guards, the administration, and the prisoners, all of whom know his conversion is genuine. If it were not, he would be readily uncovered and Tex would be exposed as a hypocrite in the sight of God and man.

In early 1976, Tex and I tape-recorded a special MESSAGE TO MANSON. The tape, which has been delivered to Manson's cell with a transcript, tells of Tex Watson's growth in the Lord and expresses the hope that Charles Manson will come to the Lord, too.

Here, in question-and-answer form, is our discussion:

Tex, you were on Death Row in San Quentin before you came down here. God delivered you from Death Row and your sentence was commuted to life in prison. Most folks expect a fellow doing a long sentence like that to be either desperate, despondent, or rebellious. Yet you are one of the most normal, happy, affirmative persons I've met. And I think Charles Manson would like to know in detail what has happened.

I got myself saved! I accepted Jesus Christ as my Lord and Savior, and now I'm just full of His light and grace, and praising Him every day.

I feel I was very fortunate. I feel it was God's plan in my life to remove the death penalty from my shoulders. But God also planned for something else to happen in my life.

I had an experience with Him back in county jail, and Charlie Manson was aware of this, but I really didn't build any foundation. I didn't build my faith upon the Rock of Jesus Christ.

The first thing that happened which I feel really drew me close to the Lord was prayers from my folks and from my friends who do know Christ. They have been behind me ever since I got into this trouble. They never have left me, and they've always been right by my side, praying for me.

But even after I read the Bible, I didn't know whether to believe in Jesus. I couldn't see Him. All of a sudden you came on the spot, and you told me about Susan Atkins, Bruce Davis and other people in prison who'd turned their lives over to the Lord. I thought, *The Lord must really be something. He's getting to all my friends.*

So I kept seeking and seeking. Then there was a revival

here at C.M.C., and that's when I really got hit by the Holy Spirit and gave my life to Jesus. I came to the conclusion God did create us and the entire world. He created everything upon this earth. There's not anything in the world He didn't create.

I praise God for His death on the Cross and for taking these sins away from me. I praise God for the opportunity to be in His plan, and for Him to have a plan for my life. I do not feel worthy, but I know by the grace of God that I am who I am, and I know I have been saved by Jesus dying upon Calvary for my sins.

I know my past has been wild, but I know now that I have accepted Christ as my Savior, that old things have passed away, and that I am a new creature in Jesus Christ. I praise God for this.

Once I fell for old Satan, and what a fool I was. I can see that. Now I'm willing to die for Jesus, just like I was willing to die for the devil. But better than that, I feel it takes a man to be able to live for Jesus, and stand up for Jesus, and to walk as He would have us walk, and follow his example here on earth by living for Him.

I know that you, Charlie, programmed me to believe in you, and to believe in the things of Satan. You brainwashed my mind, and so I was existing in a *spaced-out* state. You had me believing that's the way I could reach peace, by training myself to not believe in anything except you and drugs. But now I know I can follow Jesus as an example, and I can live a perfect life as God would have me live it.

As you study the Bible, Tex, you can see the place that prisoners have in it, and that God has a special concern for prisoners. Jesus didn't disassociate Himself from lawbreakers or sinners or prisoners. He was actually executed on Death Row.

But He came back down here and He forgave all of us, prisoners included, for our sins and mistakes. That's amazing. All through the Bible there are stories about prisoners. It's as if God paid special attention to prisoners.

I think Charles Manson would be interested in hearing about the love that's come into your life since you decided to live for Jesus.

Charlie, you wouldn't believe the kind of love I've found here in this prison. I praise God for the beautiful program we have at the chapel and the opportunity to worship. There's something happening for the Lord every night. I never found this kind of love in the Family, Charlie.

Do you find, Tex, that when Jesus Christ, with His boundless love, comes into your heart that His love isn't limited to the circle of Christian brothers who share your interest, your faith, and your concern? Do you find yourself really loving and caring for all the inmates in the prison?

Yes. I have a love for everyone that I've never been able to give before I came to know Christ. I always stayed to myself. I wouldn't come out of my cell. I was just doing my own thing. But now I know everyone in this prison, and everyone knows me. When I go by them they'll say, "What's happening?" And I'll say, "Jesus Christ is happening!" I just have so much love for all my brothers now.

I wonder how far the love of God takes you, Tex. How do you feel about the administrators in the prison? Do you hate them? Or can you love them, too?

I love everyone the same. Christ laid down the law in Matthew. He said if you get slapped on one cheek, turn the other cheek, too. That means not ever fighting back, doesn't it, Chaplain Ray? That's just humbling yourself all the way, and not only showing love to your Christian brothers who are guards and officials in the prison, but going back to those cellblocks and telling them about Jesus and the peace He can bring to their hearts.

I'm really overwhelmed by the correctional officers we have here who do know Christ and love Christ. It's just so much better when so many are going forward and striving in the same direction, with Jesus in their hearts. Things go smoothly then. It's really beautiful.

In prison, it's usually the tough who survive and the weak who are abused. And yet, to follow Christ in prison takes a lot of courage. How do you manage to be a Christian in prison?

You just stand upon the promises of Jesus, and when you feel Satan coming at you, you just rebuke him in the name of Jesus. And you use that power that you have with Jesus Christ to witness to all the prisoners you can.

I haven't had any trouble here since I accepted Christ in my heart. I've had less trouble than I had when I didn't have Him in my heart.

Many folks have the idea that lawbreakers and prisoners aren't worth much. So just lock them up and forget about them. Get them out of sight and out of mind. It's a terrible thing when a prisoner accepts that evaluation and thinks: I'm no good, my life doesn't mean anything. How does Jesus Christ make you think that you are worthy, and that your life is precious and valuable?

He did it all for us by dying for our sins on Calvary. That's the whole key to it.

Tex, did it ever occur to you, after what you've been through and the things you've been associated with, that you could come back into a good life—a happy life, where you'd be loved, where other folks could love you, and where there would be people in the free world who cared about you and prayed for you, and looked for the day when you'd be restored to freedom so you can live a good, affirmative, and worthwhile life? Did you ever dream a thing like that could happen?

I never did dream it was possible, I'll tell you! I never dreamed so much happiness could come into my life after I realized what I'd done. After I came down off drugs, and came out of the power that Satan had on me, I just thought that was the end of the road, that there was no more life, that I might as well just go ahead and die and give up. I never knew that God had this kind of power until I got to searching His Word, and the prayers of my family started being answered, and until I talked with you. Then I found out that Christ died for me, too. He didn't only die for someone who told a lie or something, but He died for everyone. He died for murderers. He died for Paul; He died for all his sins. He died for every sinner, and I praise God that through prayer and through His Word, and through my seeking, I found out Jesus died for my sins.

Tex, would you end our discussion with a prayer for all prisoners, especially Charles Manson.

Yes.

We come to You now, Jesus, just asking that You touch men's lives in institutions all over the United States. We come to You praising Your Holy Name and thanking You because we know this is within Your power, to pour Your Spirit down upon each and every man's heart. We just pray that each man will open up his heart and let Jesus in. Yes, we know You're going to come into their hearts and set them free and give them the love, peace and joy that is there when we abide in You. And we know that You can move the heart of Charlie Manson and also give him love, peace and joy. In the name of Jesus, we pray. Amen.

I'm frequently asked, "How can God forgive a man like Tex Watson who killed eight people?"

My reply relies upon Scripture. If the gospel is good news for anybody, it has to be good news for everybody. Jesus says in John 6:37, ". . . him that cometh to me I will in no wise cast out." And Isaiah 1:18 declares, ". . . though your sins be as scarlet, they shall be as white as snow; though they be red like crimson, they shall be as wool." Also, Paul's words in Romans 5:20, ". . . where sin abounded, grace did much more abound."

Tex Watson has told me, "You know, Chaplain Ray, I don't

feel that I am the person who did those crimes. When I testify, it's just like I am talking about someone else."

"You *are* talking about somebody else," I said. "The man who killed Sharon Tate and seven others doesn't live anymore. He died when you came to the Cross. Galatians 2:20 says, 'I am crucified with Christ: nevertheless I live; yet not I, but Christ liveth in me. . . .' Calvary satisfies God's demand for justice, Calvary satisfies our need for forgiveness."

Tex and I correspond frequently. He writes long, exciting letters, filled with Christian joy. The lines I treasure most from one of his letters are:

"Since coming to the Lord, I'm free mentally and free physically. These walls cease to exist and are no longer surrounding my body. A brother said to me, 'The Lord is not going to get you out of prison.' I said, 'Brother, the Lord has already got me out of prison and set me free.' "

3

The Meanest Man in Texas

He's an unlikely combination—a preacher's kid who killed four men!

Clyde Thompson, now a gentle, bespectacled man of sixty-six, is a living legend down where they grow legends by the yard. In his prime he was called *The Meanest Man in Texas.* For all I know, he may have been the meanest man in the United States. Certainly, he was a prime candidate. He was *rock-hard* and tough as leather.

Sitting in his shirtsleeves in the living room of his modest but pleasant home in Huntsville, Texas, Clyde rubs the slight stubble on the jaw of his strong, geometric face as he recounts to me his roiling, adventurous life.

He was born in Oklahoma in 1910, only three years after the Territory became the 46th state in the Union. His birthplace was the small town of Guyman, which was a refuge for desperados. Clyde's father was a Church of Christ preacher, the only man of God in the rough-and-tumble expanse where hard-cases from eight states congregated to make the area a no-man's-land. True, there was one marshal around, but he was vastly outnumbered and rendered ineffective by the preponderance of outlaws. Neither the marshal's gun nor Reverend Thompson's Bible made much of a dent in that Sodom-like part of the country at that time.

Clyde's father spent most of his life touring the early West as a circuit rider. The family moved so often, through endless towns in Texas, Arkansas, and New Mexico, that Clyde's schooling suffered. In the fourth grade, at age fourteen, he quit. "I was the oldest and dumbest kid in my class," Clyde says.

The first eighteen years of Clyde's life were peaceful and uneventful. As the son of a preacher, raised on the church bench, he never had any problems with the law until a warm, fateful day in Eastland County, Texas, in September 1928.

Clyde and two friends, who were brothers, were out coon hunting. The oldest brother, nineteen-year-old Tom, carried a shotgun. Gene, thirteen, had no gun. Clyde packed a pistol.

Tramping up a creek, they met a pair of bellicose, unfriendly men who promptly began an argument with them. Threats were shouted. The argument grew and a fight broke out.

One of the unfriendly pair carried a silver-mounted hunting horn, which he was using as a weapon, attempting to stab Tom. The other fellow had grabbed a tree limb and was beating Clyde.

Clyde lost his temper. He drew his pistol and shot the man attacking him. Clyde then turned and saw his friend Tom getting the worst of the fight with the man brandishing the hunting horn. Clyde shot him, too. Both men died at once.

For almost a generation, Clyde Thompson had sealed his fate.

Claiming self-defense at their trial, Clyde and Tom were nevertheless found guilty and sentenced to death. The third young man, tried as a juvenile, was given probation.

Errors in the transcript led to a second trial for Clyde and Tom. This time Clyde again received the death penalty, because he had fired the gun. But Tom got a five-year suspended sentence.

Awaiting transfer to Huntsville Prison for execution, Clyde was kept in the Eastland County Jail. He was soon joined by three men who'd held up a bank, one of them wearing a Santa Claus suit. A posse had given chase, and had killed the fourth man involved in the holdup.

One of the bank bandits had somehow managed to conceal a gun in his cell. With it, he shot and killed a deputy sheriff in an abortive escape attempt.

The word spread through town, and a lynch mob, five thousand strong, formed. Outside the jail, they demanded that the sheriff turn over the *sidewinder* who murdered a lawman. The sheriff refused. As the maddened crowd lunged inside the jail, the sheriff was trampled to death.

The crowd wanted more blood. They wanted Clyde Thompson's blood, even though he hadn't been involved in the killing of the deputy. The vigilantes used every one of the sheriff's thirty-two keys in an attempt to open Clyde's cell. None seemed to fit.

Another prisoner, one of the *Santa Claus* bandits, wasn't that lucky. The crowd got into his cell and hustled him down the street. Someone threw a rope over a telephone pole and tied it around his neck. Before the rope was pulled taut, the man confessed that he'd shot the deputy. The crowd left him hanging there, naked.

The next day, a new sheriff arrived. Clyde was hastily transferred to the Dallas County Jail, where years later Jack Ruby shot Lee Harvey Oswald.

On March 2, 1931, Clyde was transported to Death Row in Huntsville. He had sixty days to live. The time clicked away rapidly until he was less than two days from execution. He was given his final bath. When he had but six hours to live, he was offered his last meal, for which he had no stomach.

Then he heard the astounding, almost last-minute news. Governor Ross Sterling, reviewing the case, could see no justice in Clyde receiving the ultimate penalty while his companion got a suspended sentence. The governor felt both of them were equally guilty, but there was no way to re-try Clyde's friend Tom. With misgivings, Governor Sterling commuted Clyde's sentence to life imprisonment.

Clyde was transferred from Death Row to Huntsville's Reprieve Farm. Clyde says it was better than death, but not by much.

Prisoners chopped cotton and cleared land, working seven days a week, fourteen hours a day. Their meals consisted only of beans and sour cornbread.

"It was enough to make anyone lose his faith," says Clyde. "You just couldn't believe that God would let this happen to men if He were merciful."

Clyde's father had given him a Bible when he was on Death Row. When his father came to visit, Clyde returned it to him. "Take it," he said. "I don't believe in it anymore."

All Clyde could think of now was escape. With three others he tried his first flight for freedom, scampering off when a guard's attention was diverted by a falling tree.

The guards spotted them and one shouted, "Stop!"

Clyde and his cohorts kept running.

The guard fired and one prisoner was felled by a load of buckshot in his back. Loping along on his horse, the guard caught up to Clyde and cocked his gun. "He knew he could kill me, and I hoped he would." The guard took careful aim and fired. He shot Clyde's hat off. "All I can figure is that guard was too ornery to kill me."

For that escapade, Clyde suffered the torture of *the box.*

"As punishment they stood a prisoner up on a Coke box set on end. You would stand there for hours. I've seen men stand there until they just keeled off that thing or until they would have to move and get some circulation. But if you moved just a little, that box would jump out from beneath you, and down you'd go. Then the guard would beat you up."

Another form of torture was *the bat.* Made of rawhide with a wooden handle, it was thirty-nine inches long and two and a half inches wide. Clyde was often beaten twice a day for some real or imagined infraction of the rules. Twenty lashes was the usual punishment with the bat, which was outlawed several years ago.

"I believe the prison officials tried every means of punishment that they knew to make me straighten up, and they just made me a worse man," says Clyde. "I would have killed every one of them or anyone that got in my way trying to escape. Everybody in there knew I would do it, guard and prisoner both."

Reprieve Farm was *the* place for incorrigibles. There was no segregation of inmates. The most hardened criminals and sexual deviates were sent there, as well as the rugged first-timers.

Clyde was on the Farm for about a year when he got into

a knife fight and killed another prisoner. A year later, he was in a second knife fight and killed another inmate. In the trials that followed these killings, the only thing that saved him from the death sentence, on both occasions, was that he'd been warding off homosexual attacks.

After four additional years of peonage, marked by more escape attempts than he can remember, Clyde was moved from the jungle of the Reprieve Farm. "The reason," he says, "is because I gave them trouble all the time. They couldn't break my spirit, no matter what they did to me."

His new home was Eastham Farm, some sixteen miles northeast of Huntsville. Newly built for Clyde and only twenty-four others, was a special escape-proof cellblock dubbed *Little Alcatraz*. The place was for the most hopeless of the incorrigibles. "That's as it should have been," says Clyde. "All of us were desperate, good-for-nothing men."

Clyde and Roy Thornton, who was Bonnie Parker's husband, and two other men devised a bold plan to take over the Farm's arsenal and escape. "We planned to give guns to everyone who would shoot one," Clyde recalls.

As the break commenced, two guards and their pistols were captured. Using the guards as shields, the prisoners attempted to climb to the second floor of the arsenal.

"But they laid a trap for us and we went right into an ambush," Clyde remembers. "I was shot with a 30–30 slug through the shoulder. The powder burned and blinded me, and knocked me down. But I shook the effects off enough to get up."

In the exchange of fire, one of the four prisoners was killed. Clyde and the two others were still battling it out. Clyde kept shooting until the chamber of his gun clicked empty. Only then was he overpowered. So, finally, were the others. The guards somehow escaped without a scratch.

Clyde's shoulder had been gouged by a ferocious steel-wadded, hollow-nosed bullet. Several bones were shattered. An operation removed all the lead the doctor could find, but Clyde's still walking around today with lead encapsulated in his body, a souvenir of the *Little Alcatraz* break.

Unable to raise his right arm, Clyde was still sent back to work after thirty days.

"I just lived, dreamed, and schemed about escaping. From one day to the next, I didn't intend to be in prison. If a guard so much as turned his head, I was going to be gone."

Clyde was in *Little Alcatraz* for eight months when a prisoner was knifed to death. "They automatically blamed me since they didn't know who did it," Clyde says.

He was charged with his third prison killing and indicted for the fifth time for murder.

"I knew who killed the man. Everyone in *Little Alcatraz* knew who killed him. But nobody would tell, least of all I, who was the meanest one of all."

A day before he was scheduled to go on trial for the fatal knifing, the case against Clyde Thompson was dismissed for lack of evidence.

"If they could have found two false witnesses against me, I wouldn't be here today. But I was in with men who'd have died rather than tell the prison officials anything."

Never reluctant to *fess up* to a crime, Clyde says he was innocent of this one. "A good friend of mine, who was mentally ill, killed the man."

At this juncture, Clyde wasn't paranoid. Still and all he had reason to feel he was being unjustly persecuted. The state of Texas had tried to electrocute him for two killings in which there were important mitigating circumstances, two other killings where self-defense was clear, and one killing he had nothing to do with. And he hadn't forgotten being nearly lynched for another killing of which he was innocent.

Small wonder he developed the reputation as *The Meanest Man in Texas.* Some folks said he was too mean to die.

After the *Little Alcatraz* killing, Clyde refused to work in the fields, because he figured the guards would probably shoot him in the back if they had the chance.

The response of Huntsville authorities to Clyde's rebellion was unique—he was literally imprisoned in a morgue.

When inmates had been executed, or had died, their bodies were stored in a building known as the *Old Morgue* behind

Death Row. The Morgue was a poured concrete structure with six slabs inside it for caskets. There was only a one-foot-square window which shone stingy beams of light for five hours a day. There was no running water and no light fixtures. Clyde was allowed no eating utensils—not even a spoon. The officials were afraid he would sharpen it and kill himself. All his clothes were removed except a pair of shorts. He received one daily bucket of cold water, and ate his worm-laden chili with his hands.

Living like an animal, Clyde spent a year and a half in the *Morgue*. Finally, to keep from going stir mad he asked a guard for a Bible. "I had nothing better to do, so I thought I'd occupy my mind. I'd never paid any attention to my father's preaching and I'd never really read the Bible. I'd heard that the Bible was filled with contradictions. I set out to find the inconsistencies."

However, there were none.

"The more I studied the Bible, the more convinced I became that it was a Book of truth, and I was false. I read it through many times, verse by verse, chapter by chapter. And I came to realize that this was actually the Word of God and the only hope for man in this world.

"I repented, got down on my hands and knees, and asked God if He would save a worthless wretch like me. Maybe, I wondered, there was some way He could use me for His honor and glory.

"God's answer came back like a rifle shot. 'Yes,' God said."

When he began studying the Bible, Clyde couldn't spell the most common words correctly. He used a wall of the *Morgue* as a blackboard.

"I would write down words from the Bible, then study and memorize them. From the Bible to the wall to my mind became the pattern of my study."

Clyde's life swiftly took on a new dimension, noticeable by the guards who brought his food, the guard who escorted him for his weekly bath, and the man who shaved him once a week.

"They realized they had a changed man in Clyde Thompson! I wasn't 'The Meanest Man in Texas' anymore. I was just a new child of Jesus. I didn't even resent all the lost time

in prison. One of my favorite passages from Scripture is Joel
2:25: 'And I will restore to you the years that the locust hath
eaten. . . .' "

Clyde's behavior had changed so drastically that he was
allowed a few small privileges. A single light was put into the
Morgue. Then running water. And then a radio.

The Huntsville administration encouraged Clyde in his Bible studies. He was permitted to enroll in Lee College's two-
year correspondence Bible and journalism courses. Soon he was
writing poetry and articles for religious newspapers.

After five and a half years in the *Morgue,* he was moved to
Shamrock, a large isolation unit for about four hundred men.
Two years later he was working as the prison chaplain's book-
keeper and was teaching an eighty-one-member Bible class. His
witnessing to other prisoners resulted in more than twenty of
them accepting Christ.

Clyde, after spending more than a quarter of a century in
penitentiaries, was released in November 1955. His wife,
Julia, was there to meet him at the gate. They'd met and
fallen in love after corresponding for about a year. Julia had
seen Clyde's picture in the newspapers and read his story.
She always believed that Clyde wasn't as mean as his reputation. After their marriage in prison, Julia was indefatigable in
her appearances before the parole board. "Look at the man
and not his record," she urged, and finally the parole board
listened.

In the years since his release, Clyde Thompson has remained
close to the Lord. He has his own prison ministry. He's built
a guest house on his lot expressly for released prisoners who are
rootless. Clyde helps them get on their feet when they leave
Huntsville. Though his resources are meager, he provides them
with what financial help he can. He also helps them get jobs
and gives them encouragement. "I just say if I made it with
the Lord's help, you can make it too with the help of the Lord.
He's there for anyone to reach out and grab hold of."

Recently Clyde took me on a trip to a cemetery. As we
walked among the headstones, he said, "This is a special ceme-

tery. Prisoners from Huntsville called it Peckerwood Hill, though it's been renamed Captain Joe Byrd Cemetery. It's the potter's field of the Bible and the Boot Hill of the Old West."

The cemetery holds the bodies of many of the men who were executed at Huntsville. Carved on each headstone is the prisoner's name, the date of his execution, the abbreviation EX (for EXECUTED), and a number.

Clyde swings his glance to a grave marked: Richard Johnson, May 15, 1933, EX 82.

Then his eyes hold for a long moment on the stone that reads: *Monous Twitty, April 24, 1934,* EX *84.*

Says Clyde: "My execution number was EX 83. They never got a chance to use it, thanks to Jesus Christ."

4

Forgotten Justice

The finger of God, very early in the Bible, indelibly etched the Ten Commandments on two tablets of stone. He gave the Commandments to Moses as dramatically as possible to emphasize the importance of law and justice. Says Exodus 19:18: "And Mount Sinai was altogether on a smoke, because the Lord descended upon it in fire: and the smoke thereof ascended as the smoke of a furnace, and the whole mount quaked greatly." Obviously, law and justice were not idle matters to God.

The Commandments, amplified throughout the Bible by a detailed code of right and wrong, are still the *alpha* and *omega* of every civilized nation in the world. Where the Commandments do not hold sway, anarchy, barbarism and blasphemy rule. Only to the extent that a nation obeys the laws of God is there an opportunity for an orderly society where men and women may pursue happiness, engage in fruitful labor, and receive the inspiration of worship.

In our thermonuclear age, in this time of unprecedented technology, it has been forgotten that the Bible offers a stern, swift, fair and effective system of justice. That ignoble forgetfulness and the compromising of biblical law have caused America to pay a fearful price.

From 1960 to 1969 crime increased by 148 percent. Since then the rate has accelerated even faster! Crime has become a way of life for an ever growing army of lawbreakers, and the streets of America have become a jungle.

The situation in Berkeley, California, is all too typical. More than two hundred people in one neighborhood have formed a citizens patrol to supplement the undermanned police department. Similar patrols exist in every major American city, including affluent Beverly Hills, California, where the average family income is twenty-five thousand dollars a year.

The Berkeley self-protection group was formed in response to four murders, eighteen robberies, and seven rapes in a period of a month.

One victimized family answered a knock on the door to find a man with a gun. The intruder instantly shot and killed the mother and her two small children.

Another family was ordered to strip at gunpoint, and the wife, a teacher, was raped in front of her husband and son.

The sale of deadbolt locks is way up, and now people leave their porch lights on all night.

Berkeley citizens' organizing to protect themselves is particularly significant, since the community is considered liberal. One resident concluded: "What's going on here is part of the liberal confusion. People are torn between their hatred for the police and their desire for safety. And you can't have it both ways." Another resident added: "We live in a condition of terror, and fear immobilizes people. I'm afraid things are going to get worse before they get better, if they ever get better."

Until there is a vast law-and-order reform movement, based on divine justice, things will not get better.

The number of Americans incarcerated in federal and state prisons has soared 10.5 percent, to a new total of a quarter million—the largest prisoner population in the nation's history. And the end is nowhere in sight.

According to Neal R. Pierce, of *The National Journal,* "Prison building threatens to become the biggest growth industry of the 1970's. With prisons across the nation already grievously overcrowded, 524 new facilities or expansions are now on the drawing boards. Their likely cost: more than $4 billion."

Vast, expensive prisons are a relatively late invention of mankind; they did not begin to appear until the late 1200's in England.

In the biblical epoch, there was no need for large prisons. Imprisonment wasn't used as a penalty. The secret of the wise ancients for avoiding prisons and dealing realistically with crime was two-fold: swift justice and restitution.

Lawbreakers were quickly brought before judges who meted out punishment immediately. It was a very direct type of punishment, which intimately involved the criminal and his victim. There were no loopholes or such delaying tactics by clever lawyers as endless postponements and appeals. The only appeal for the malefactor, if he intended to mend his ways, was to God.

In the Old Testament, when a man committed a crime, he wasn't sent to a prison to be fed and sheltered at the expense of other people.

God's law was clear.

Exodus 22:1 declares: "If a man shall steal an ox, or a sheep, and kill it, or sell it; he shall restore five oxen for an ox, and four sheep for a sheep."

Again and again in the Old Testament the point is made about restitution:

Exodus 22:4: "If the theft be certainly found in his hand alive, whether it be ox, or ass, or sheep; he shall restore double."

Exodus 22:6: "If a fire break out, and catch in thorns, so that the stacks of corn, or the standing corn, or the field, be consumed therewith; he that kindled the fire shall surely make restitution."

Exodus 22:7: "If a man shall deliver unto his neighbour money or stuff to keep, and it be stolen out of the man's house; if the thief be found, let him pay double."

The tradition persisted in the New Testament. Zacchaeus, a dishonest tax collector before he was converted by Jesus, tells the Lord in Luke 19:8, ". . . if I have taken anything from any man by false accusation, I restore him fourfold."

With this system of restitution, the victim didn't lose. The taxpayer didn't lose. The loser was the criminal.

What if the criminal couldn't repay? In that case he was required to sell himself as a bondservant to the man he had wronged or to another employer-master who would pay off his obligation, and he had to work for that person until he paid the debt. Such was the "imprisonment" of the Bible.

The methodology allowed people in biblical times to maintain an orderly society. There was a minimum amount of crime and taxes. Exactly the opposite characterizes our society today.

From Exodus to Revelation, the criminal was punished severely but evenhandedly. Under our contemporary system those who pay the least for their crimes are criminals.

Despite overcrowded prisons and rising inmate population, Mayor Thomas Maloney of Wilmington, Delaware, observes, "The tragedy is that citizens are now the prisoners in their homes, with chains, locks, bars and grates while the criminals are on the outside, roaming free."

The great need is to change and entirely restructure the way society deals with crime. The model should be the Bible. We need desperately to recall and recreate its procedures. With an ever growing crime problem and a $4 billion bill for new prisons looming ahead, how much longer can we afford to forget the precepts of biblical justice?

Instead of penalizing the victim and the taxpayer, crime should be paid for by the criminals. We need less retribution and more restitution.

Suppose a man is convicted of committing a $5,000 armed robbery, and is sentenced to five years imprisonment with no restitution required. The money he stole is repaid by the victim or his insurance company, which results in higher premium rates for everyone. The taxpayer, who had no part in the crime, pays all the legal charges, the cost of investigation, arrest and trial. (At the time of her conviction for bank robbery, the bill to Californians for housing, trying and hospitalizing Patricia Hearst was in excess of $230,000.) Keeping the man in prison will cost at least $5,000 a year. Moreover, the man's family will probably apply for welfare, an additional taxpayer burden.

The result of this system is that the criminal is only inconvenienced while at the same time he is housed, clothed, fed and given free medical attention. That isn't justice, it's merely a form of comparatively mild retribution or punishment and it serves nobody well. The system totally ignores the victims and the taxpayers.

If the thief had been sentenced to repay the money he stole, three things would have resulted. First, the victim would be compensated. Second, the taxpayer would be relieved of a major part of the cost of the crime. Third, the lawbreaker would learn more and be more effectively rehabilitated by making restitution.

The rule of restitution should not apply only to those who steal with a gun, but those who rob with a ballpoint pen or a computer. Christ dealt with the white-collar criminals of His time, denouncing the moneychangers and overturning their tables for charging double interest.

America, according to the Justice Department, is buckling under the weight of $50 billion a year stolen by white-collar crooks (far, far more than is amassed by armed criminals). Rarely, if ever, is any of that $50 billion repaid when the "businessmen" in custom-tailored suits are convicted.

In July 1974, C. Arnholt Smith, a San Diego, California, financier, was charged with twenty-five counts of fraud after the collapse of his U.S. National Bank. Smith pleaded no contest to four of the federal charges. He was placed on probation and fined a token $30,000. The indictments had alleged that he stole more than $60 million from his own bank!

Stanley Goldblum, the forty-eight-year-old former chairman of Los Angeles-based Equity Funding Corporation of America was responsible for the largest theft in American corporate history, a $2 billion assignation of assets, a sum that far exceeds the $1,351,128,000 assessed valuation of the entire city of Pittsburgh, Goldblum's birthplace.

Until 1973, Equity had been in the business of selling mutual funds and insurance policies to investors. Then two disgruntled former employees began talking to government investigators, who were astonished to learn that with the help of a busy computer, the company had manufactured more than sixty thousand phony insurance policies, many in the names of dead people. A startling two-thirds of all its policies were spurious. Thousands of man-in-the-street investors had been bilked.

Pending trial, Goldblum, living in a $495,000 mansion, had no difficulty posting bail of $200,000.

Shortly after his trial began, Goldblum, facing a thirty-year sentence but a maximum fine of only $31,000, pleaded guilty.

The judge's sentence was eight years, and not a nickel in restitution. The fine wasn't even demanded. Goldblum, eligible for parole after serving one-third of his term, will presumably return to his mansion, still, presumably, a multimillionaire.

Here and there in our society a start toward the principle of restitution has been made:

Federal Judge Miles W. Lord in 1976 demanded that six drug companies, convicted of overcharging and price fixing, return $40 million to 885,000 people.

"There has never been a case like it and may never be again," says columnist Nicholas von Hoffman wryly. "Judge Lord's conduct leaves him vulnerable to removal on the grounds of gross competence and excessive fairness."

In Minnesota, two new restitution programs are in force for the victims of such crimes as forgery, fraud, and theft.

The Minnesota Restitution Center (for men) and the Property Offenders Program (for women) allow prisoners convicted of these crimes to leave jail after serving only a few months on condition that they repay the money they stole. As in the biblical era, they must negotiate, often face-to-face, with their victims.

The programs are working splendidly, and every state in the nation should follow the example of Minnesota. Every magistrate should also follow the example of Judge Lord (a most appropriate name).

The penology of the Bible doesn't rely alone on restitution, but on work as well.

We need to develop a creative alternative to prisons. For the most part, imprisonment should be limited to incorrigibly violent criminals. Society, obviously, needs that protection. But even those prisoners should be allowed the therapy of labor.

All inmates in our penal institutions, except the sick and infirm, should be made productive.

One corrections officer in a large prison told me: "The normal life of an inmate is sixteen hours a day of lusting and eight hours a day of sleeping."

That's the situation in virtually all our prisons.

Penitentiaries should no longer be used as storage warehouses for human beings. Idleness breeds trouble and restlessness behind the walls, as it does outside the walls. The necessity is to reintroduce the Bible's bondservant concept. The entire apparatus of justice must be refocused. In most cases, those convicted of crimes should be sent to prison only if they refuse to take a job and compensate their victims.

Inside prison, inmates should be required to work at meaningful tasks, and they should be paid prevailing wages. What they earn should be shared by those they victimized and the prisoners' families (in order to help reduce the nation's astronomical welfare bill).

Private industry and governmental agencies should farm out as much work as possible to prisons. Every state governor should appoint a tough, no-nonsense task force to determine in detail what profit-making businesses can be created in its prisons. The prisons should become anvils of labor, factories employing men rather than merely overseeing them.

The work-furlough program in some California prisons should be vastly expanded and copied by other states. Under that program, minimum security prisoners and those soon to be released are permitted to leave the institution in the morning, put in a full day's work as free men in the free world, then return at night.

The need for upgrading education inside prisons is vast. Inmates should be taught realistic vocational or white-collar skills that will be in demand when they leave the institution. This would do much to reduce the high rate of repeat offenders and serve to rehabilitate the 95 percent of prisoners who will return to society. We must be concerned with what kind of people inmates are going to be when they leave prison. Certainly, if they have worked productively, they will be better citizens. And if they have had an experience with Christ through the spreading of the gospel by prison chaplains or by volunteer ministries such as mine, chances are they will become model citizens when they are freed. The rate of recidivism is at least two-thirds lower among Christians coming out of prison than among non-Christians who are released.

Jesus says in Matthew 25:36, ". . . I was in prison, and ye came unto me." He was stressing helpfulness, sympathy, good works, compassion, brotherly love, and saying that visiting prisoners and winning their souls are the obligations of Christians.

That spirit is the full thrust of my ministry.

The Bible doesn't take the view that lawbreakers should be treated with maudlin sentimentality by Christians. The Bible takes the view that even though men and women have sinned and broken the law, they are still members of the human family. Their lives are precious.

All men are created in the image of God and are capable of redemption by the blood of the Son of God. No matter how ugly a man's life has been, no matter what crimes he's committed, if that man can be reached with the gospel and turned to Christ, he is a new creature.

My ministry is in no way related to the misguided liberals who still talk in hazy, unspecific language about the rehabilitation of prisoners; who assume that lawbreakers should not be punished because they are the victims of an unjust society that did not create an ideal environment in which they have no inclination, need or desire to commit criminal acts.

I flatly and fully reject that thesis. It is not only unbiblical but contrary to reality.

Man was created by an intelligent, moral, spiritual, and intellectual God who gave each individual the power to choose. Man, therefore, is not the product of his environment. He is the product of his own choices.

Society does not owe a man a living. Nothing is further from the truth. Every man owes it to himself to work for a living.

In my own family of ten—my father, mother and my seven brothers and sisters—there was sufficient poverty to start a national crime wave. But nothing of that kind happened. No one in our family was ever sentenced to a day in jail. We were taught that the remedy for poverty wasn't crime but work.

If poverty was the cause of crime, the poorest countries in the world would have the highest rate of crime, and the richest nations would have the least crime. But exactly the opposite is true. There is more crime per capita in the United States than in most nations in Asia and Africa. If poverty caused crime, millions upon millions of Americans who came from ghettos, instead of being hard working, useful and God-fearing citizens, would be in jail.

Crime stems from the human heart. The Bible teaches that murder and villainy come from inside a man. That's why Solomon said in Proverbs 4:23, "Keep thy heart with all diligence; for out of it are the issues of life." Until the hearts of men can be changed through Christ they will continue to kill, rape, steal and embezzle.

Thus my ministry puts its major emphasis on curing the human heart of the virus of crime. When the heart is changed, the crime disappears.

Time and again I have seen that the human heart can be changed, that great sinners can become great Christians once they have met the Lord and received the transforming experience of salvation.

Perhaps no better illustration of that verity can be found than in the story of the man who was once the nation's most notorious outlaw. . . .

5
Public Enemy Number 1

Have you been to Jesus for the cleansing power?
Are you washed in the blood of the Lamb?
Are you fully trusting in His grace this hour?
Are you washed in the blood of the Lamb?

Her sloping jaw set tautly, her eyes dark caves of fear, Mrs. Alice Hamilton softly hummed the words to that venerable and vigorous hymn in the living room of her small frame house in West Dallas, Texas, on the evening of May 10, 1935. She remembered that she had often sung "Are You Washed in the Blood?" to her sons Floyd and Raymond when they were children. Now her sons were no longer children. Both had been members of the Bonnie and Clyde gang. And both were imprisoned. Floyd was in the penitentiary at Leavenworth, Kansas, and Raymond, the younger brother, was about to be executed in the electric chair.

It was almost 9 P.M. Mrs. Hamilton walked to a small, waist-high table, and with a quavering hand flicked the radio on, adjusted the sound, and waited for the announcer's punishing words. They came shortly, tumbling and ricocheting into the room like a tornado. "Raymond Hamilton has just been pronounced dead by officials of the state prison at Huntsville, Texas."

Mrs. Hamilton's entire body went limp. She closed her eyes and prayed for the soul of her son.

"I was born in a Christian home and taught that daily prayer is a cleanser for the mind," Mrs. Hamilton would say several years later. "I was taught to love and honor God and that hard work is good for the soul. And that's what I taught my sons."

Yet Mrs. Hamilton went to her grave never knowing quite what had gone wrong in the lives of Floyd and Raymond. Perhaps it was the fact that her husband had deserted her when the boys and their four sisters were young. Perhaps it was an accident of geography—her sons had grown up in the same neighborhood as Bonnie Parker and Clyde Barrow. Floyd had confided to her, "Clyde Barrow says he's killed thirteen people, ten of them police officers."

Mrs. Hamilton also went to her grave with a singular, unwanted distinction. "As far as I know," she once told a reporter, "no other mother has ever suffered the agonizing experience of raising *two Public Enemies Number 1*. I pray that none ever will."

> Are you walking daily by the Saviour's side?
> Are you washed in the blood of the Lamb?
> Do you rest each moment with the Crucified?
> Are you washed in the blood of the Lamb?

Today, when he's in church or alone, the words to his mother's favorite hymn spill frequently from the lips of sixty-eight-year-old Floyd Hamilton. The last survivor of the Bonnie and Clyde gang, Floyd, his brief but spectacular, bullet-dodging career of crime behind him, is one of the finest servants of the Lord I know.

Sitting in the same room where his mother heard the news of his brother's execution, Floyd recounted to me his crime-to-Christ saga.

His and Bonnie Parker's family moved to the West Dallas area the same year, 1920. Clyde Barrow arrived in 1922.

"We were friends for as long as I can remember. Bonnie was a fun-loving girl. She took part in all kinds of recreation and school activities. But Clyde was the reverse. He didn't take part in any school activities. He'd stand up against the wall, or over by the fence, and watch everyone else. But still he was a person who would go out of his way to do small favors for folks, and make friends or be friendly.

"Clyde's lawbreaking came on gradually. The Barrow family had to live in an old campgrounds because their daddy didn't have any work. I think Clyde and some of his brothers started picking up things to help out a little bit. He was just a kid when he was arrested for burglary, and sentenced to fourteen years in prison."

Paroled after three years, Clyde tried working for a living. "He did jobs at various places, but two police officers found out where he was working, and they went out and told his employers that he was an ex-convict, and that he would probably steal from them. So they fired him."

"Then," says Floyd, "the police kept arresting Clyde and putting him in jail anytime there was a crime committed within fifty miles of where he was standing. Finally, Clyde decided to just hit the road as a full-time lawbreaker. My brother went with him. Raymond was Clyde Barrow's first crime partner."

They robbed a Texas meat-packing company and fled to Oklahoma. There, in the course of another robbery, a police officer was killed. Clyde and Raymond sped back to Dallas to pick up Bonnie Parker. Floyd Hamilton watched them drive off in a brand-new stolen car.

The trio found refuge at a ranch in New Mexico, but they made one mistake. "In those days," says Floyd, "anyone who had a new car was considered very well off."

A police officer, driving by the ranch, spotted the car and decided to investigate. Bonnie Parker met the officer at the door. Clyde and Raymond sneaked around the back and with guns drawn took the officer prisoner. They drove to San Antonio, across the state line, where they released the officer unharmed. That escapade resulted in federal kidnapping charges against Clyde, Bonnie and Raymond. Clyde and Raymond were already wanted for murdering the officer in Oklahoma.

"From then on," Floyd sighs, "their crime career just snow-balled. Mine too, I guess."

> When the Bridegroom cometh will your robes be white?
> Are you washed in the blood of the Lamb?
> Will your soul be ready for the mansions bright?
> And be washed in the blood of the Lamb?

"I wasn't nearly ready for Jesus," Floyd adds. "I went the path of sin, getting more and more involved."

The police were keeping the Dallas homes of Bonnie and Clyde under close surveillance. The police suspected—cor-rectly—that Floyd was in touch with the outlaws. Because of Floyd's help, Bonnie and Clyde did elude police whenever they came to Dallas, which was frequently. Floyd Hamilton was the only man in Dallas County that Clyde Barrow trusted. The trust was justified. Floyd, though he was being watched him-self, managed to set up clandestine meetings between Bonnie and Clyde and their families on country back roads and in secluded farmhouses.

Shortly before Bonnie and Clyde were killed, Clyde asked Floyd Hamilton to act as a go-between with the authorities. Floyd didn't hesitate to put himself in jeopardy, openly admit-ting his link to Bonnie and Clyde.

Clyde's offer was to give up the Barrow gang, including William (Deacon) Jones, another childhood pal from West Dallas, if the states of Texas and Oklahoma and FBI Director J. Edgar Hoover would agree to give them life sentences. The lawmen refused to make a deal.

Now things began to happen fast. Clyde Barrow and Bonnie Parker were gunned to death—and into the realm of legend—near Gibsland, Louisiana on May 23, 1934. Soon afterwards, Raymond Hamilton was taken into cus-tody after a shoot-out with Texas Rangers in Dallas. Before he could be extradited to Oklahoma to face a murder charge, Raymond and three other convicts managed a suc-cessful break from Huntsville Prison. The escape cost one guard his life. Raymond was named by the FBI as *Public Enemy Number 1* and was quickly recaptured. He was tried and convicted as an accessory to murder. He hadn't fired the bullet that resulted in the guard's death, but he still was sentenced to the electric chair for that crime. Meantime, early in 1935, Floyd Hamilton was charged with harboring Bonnie and Clyde on eighty-one occasions. He was given two years in Leavenworth.

Floyd says he was fortunate. He came whistle-thin close to following his brother to the electric chair. A farmer named Floyd as the killer of two policemen on a road outside Dallas. Floyd, who knew the farmer slightly, was identified by him because there was a reward posted for the killer of the officers. The story made headlines for several weeks in the Dallas newspapers. Floyd owes his life, he says, to a police ballistics expert who discovered that the guns used to kill the officers were owned by Bonnie and Clyde.

"They dropped the indictment. But if that farmer had testified against me, I'd be dead now. It would have been his word against mine. Any jury, because of my known connection with Bonnie and Clyde and because everyone knew my brother had been executed, would have believed him."

Floyd stares ruefully out the window of his modest home. He shakes his head sadly.

"By the time I was paroled from Leavenworth, they were all dead and gone. Bonnie. Clyde. My brother. In the beginning I don't think that we were really any different from anyone else, but I suppose circumstances got us into trouble. Actually we got into deep trouble without intending to. Soon we got into trouble so far that we didn't see any place to turn back. Still, I should have known better. What happened to Bonnie and Clyde and Raymond should have taught me a lesson. But it didn't work out that way, though I tried."

Floyd got a job as a pipe fitter at an oil refinery near Vivian, Louisiana. It lasted twenty months. Then Floyd returned to Dallas.

"The first time I went to town I was arrested. The police said

I was robbing and stealing. The same thing happened to me as to Clyde Barrow. Anytime some kind of crime was committed anywhere in the county, they put me in jail and held me as long as they could without any evidence.

"Even while I was serving the two years in Leavenworth, the Dallas authorities charged me with robbing a bank and the attempted murder of a police officer! Can you imagine. I had to face preliminary hearings on those charges when I got out of prison. Finally, when they realized they couldn't frame me or that their case was ridiculous—I don't know which—they dropped the whole thing."

But the Dallas police, according to Floyd, wouldn't leave him alone. Soon he was arrested for receiving and concealing stolen merchandise.

"The fact is, I had loaned my car to one of my brothers-in-law, who wanted to use it to drive to Houston. On the road, just outside Dallas, he was flagged down for speeding. The police found that there was a stolen tire on the car. I don't know who put it there, but it wasn't me.

"My brother-in-law was told that if he would testify that I helped steal the tire, they would turn him loose. And that's what he did. So they came and put me in jail."

That occurred in 1937, shortly before Christmas. Though it was a relatively minor charge, Floyd was refused bail. Floyd then determined that he would bail himself out of confinement. Telling the jailer he was hungry, Floyd asked him to bring in a large box of soda crackers from a grocery store near the jail. The box, Floyd knew, couldn't be slipped through the bars because it was too big. The plan worked. When the jailer returned, he opened Floyd's cell. Floyd, a prisoner named Ted Walters and another man overpowered the guard, took his keys and locked the jailer in their cell. To keep the authorities busy, Floyd opened all the cell doors and turned loose everybody who wanted to go.

Floyd and "Terrible Ted" Walters, as he was soon called by the press, began their crime spree. They'd discussed it in jail, and found they were of a single mind. Ted Walters was a congenital criminal, and Floyd figured he might as well become the hardcore lawbreaker everyone thought he was.

"That was the most miserable life I ever lived, worse than prison. People, especially a lot of youngsters these days, think that being on the road and violating the law whenever you want to, has a mess of glamor to it. That's not true."

Floyd says that he and Ted could only sleep with one eye open, that they were constantly looking over their shoulders. They were constantly in hiding, and whenever possible, they traveled at night.

"You always wondered when you saw someone looking at you a second time if that person recognized you and would report your whereabouts to the police. You were jeopardizing your life every minute that you were out there. It was horrible. If only I had realized then that I'd be safe in the arms of Jesus."

> Lay aside the garments that are stained with sin,
> And be washed in the blood of the Lamb.
> There's a fountain flowing for the soul unclean,
> O be washed in the blood of the Lamb.

Floyd and Ted robbed indiscriminately—banks, stores, a ballpark. "Once we robbed a place down in East Texas—one of these places where trucks picked up oil. We got jumped very quickly by the police and barely got away, a shower of lead chasing us out of town."

On those occasions when they did talk to people, his partner, says Floyd, had a habit of bragging that he was a criminal. "But instead of giving them his own name, Ted always claimed he was Floyd Hamilton." As a result, Floyd got all the publicity. Soon any crime committed in the Southwest was attributed to him.

"How long did your crime spree continue?" I asked Floyd.

"From the first part of 1938 until we got caught in the fall. It was less than a year, but in that time I'd become *Public Enemy Number One.*"

Floyd received swift justice. He was sentenced to fifty-five years in prison on a variety of charges, including armed robbery and violating the Dyer Act (interstate transportation of stolen cars). Fortunately, in the dozens of holdups he'd committed, no one was killed. On November 5, 1938, less than two months after he was caught, Floyd was back in Leavenworth. A few weeks later, the warden sent for him and accused him of planning an escape. Floyd denied this. Nevertheless, Floyd was transferred to *The Hole*, an isolation cell. He found that he had a famous neighbor. "I was in Cell 13 and Robert Stroud, the *Birdman of Alcatraz*, had two cells, 9 and 10."

Floyd says that Robert Stroud was a loner and every bit as tough as his reputation. He hated men but loved canaries. Stroud had been sentenced to twelve years for killing a bartender in Alaska. Inexplicably, just before his sentence was completed, Stroud entered the Leavenworth mess hall on a day in March 1916 and, before twelve hundred convicts and prison officials, stabbed and killed guard Andrew F. Turner.

The reason for the killing was never adequately explained, but Stroud did tell Floyd Hamilton: "The guard took sick and died all of a sudden. He died of heart trouble. I guess you would call it a puncture of the heart. I never have given any reason for doing it, so they won't have much to work on; only that I killed him, and that won't do much good. I admit that much."

Stroud was convicted and sentenced to die on the gallows which were constructed in the exercise yard not more than two hundred feet from his cell.

The reputation Stroud had built up as a lover of canaries and an expert on their diseases stood him in good stead. In 1920, after four years of appeals had been exhausted, his mother in a last, desperate hope went to see President Woodrow Wilson, who commuted her son's sentence to life in solitary confinement. The commutation came just eight days before Stroud was scheduled to die.

"They tore the walls down between two cells to let Stroud study his birds," says Floyd. "It was in Leavenworth that

Stroud got his nickname, *The Birdman.* The author who wrote his story called it *The Birdman of Alcatraz.* I suppose he thought he'd sell more books that way since Alcatraz had such an awful reputation.

"Stroud never had a single bird in Alcatraz. I guess I ought to know. We had cells next to each other when I was in solitary there."

Floyd was sent to Alcatraz after serving ten years at Leavenworth. Stroud followed a short time later. *The Birdman* and Floyd Hamilton weren't the only well-known criminals on the Rock at that time. Alcatraz held a who's who of American felons, including Scarface Al Capone, Machine Gun Kelly, Alvin Karpis, and two of Ma Barker's sons.

Though Alcatraz had an escape-proof reputation, Floyd tried bolting to freedom every chance he got.

"I was determined that I wasn't going to live out my life on that rock."

Floyd's most notable escape attempt took place in the winter of 1942. He and three other prisoners, after cutting the bars to their cell, made it into the water in San Francisco Bay.

"The man with me was shot to death beside me in the water. His body was never recovered. The other two were retaken shortly after the escape. I found out later that the prison doctor and a guard who were watching the chase from the top of a building reported they saw me go down in a hail of bullets."

Clyde found a cave and stayed there for three days, burying himself under a pile of old truck tires. He considered swimming the mile to the mainland, but the choppy water was too formidable a barrier.

Exhausted, with his last ounce of strength, Floyd finally made his way from the cave back to the grounds of Alcatraz. The astonished authorities, believing he was dead, found him asleep.

Floyd became a hero to the six hundred men who were imprisoned with him in the Bay fortress. The warden was less charitable. For punishment, Floyd was sent to *The Hole.*

"They took all my clothes. The first twenty-one days they fed me nothing but bread and water. The cell was dark, with a metal floor. No bed. No chair. No furnishings of any kind. At night I slept between two thin blankets. I thought I would freeze to death."

Floyd toughed out his time in *The Hole,* which is located on the bottom floor of dungeon-like *D Block* (reserved for the most dangerous men in Alcatraz) by dreaming of another escape attempt. When he was transferred to the top tier of *D Block,* he soon tried to cut his way out again, using razor blades to carve a hole in the ceiling. He was caught, and moved to an escape-proof cell on the second tier. The inmate in the next cell was an old acquaintance from Leavenworth, Robert Stroud (who died in prison of natural causes in 1963). There was only a thin strip of metal separating the cells occupied by Floyd and Stroud.

Stroud was still bitter and said little. He wasn't pleasant company. But an inmate named Stewart, who was in the other cell adjoining Floyd's, was worse company.

Stewart spent his days endlessly pacing his cell. He cursed everything and everyone for his predicament. He was doing very hard time. Soon Floyd began to emulate Stewart, striding the three-step length of his cell and berating God and man for consigning him to a fate that was living hell.

Stewart developed bleeding ulcers. "So did I," says Floyd. "That really scared me. I knew that if Stewart couldn't do his short sentence of only seven years, I would surely never be able to live out the rest of my term, more than forty years.

"Stewart died of a perforated ulcer, burning up on the inside, pacing his cage until the last like a wild animal."

After that, Floyd began to respond to the efforts of the three people who were trying to help him, his mother, Mrs. Hattie Rankin, a dedicated Christian lady from Dallas interested in reforming prisoners through Jesus, and Dr. W.A. Criswell, who journeyed to Alcatraz from the First Baptist Church in Dallas to visit Floyd.

By letter and in face-to-face conversations, all three had the same message for Floyd.

"They told me I could put the bars of Alcatraz behind me if I changed my way of living. They urged me to let God solve my problems, and told me that I should turn my life and my problems over to Him."

Have you been to Jesus for the cleansing power?
Are you washed in the blood of the Lamb?
Are you fully trusting in His grace this hour?
Are you washed in the blood of the Lamb?

"My first idea," Floyd continued, "was to use God. I thought that if all you had to do to get out of prison was just pray, well, that wasn't too bad.

"I even asked God to help me escape. I figured that with God's muscles and my brains I could get out of there.

"You see, I had a God that I had made up in my own image. I thought that whatever I considered as just, He would do. I told Him to go and see all the folks that had done me a lot of damage, and punish them, at least until I got out, and got there myself to finish up the job.

"I thought I was praying to an Old Man God, seated on a throne; that Jesus was at His right hand, saying, 'This Floyd Hamilton is a pretty good old boy. So answer his prayer.'

"I thought God had angels and saints over on the left-hand side, singing His praises and keeping Him in good humor. I thought if I could catch God in a good humor, and get Jesus to intercede, I would get out!"

When nothing happened, Floyd began to re-examine his beliefs about God. He started reading the Bible and came to a new understanding of how the power of God works.

"I wondered why some people had found God, and I couldn't get an answer from Him," Floyd says. "Then I realized that when a person really gets sincere, he finds out that he's the one who must condition himself to receive God's blessings. The fault is not in God at all. You do not change God's mind. You have to change your own mind. You have to start working on yourself. That's something most people never do."

Floyd now looked at himself more objectively.

"I saw that I wasn't such a great guy after all.

"I saw that it wasn't everyone else who was to blame for my troubles. It was me! I had to straighten myself up, and straighten myself out. When I started to do that, I discovered that God was doing great things for me, and that He *had* done great things for me!"

> Are you walking daily by the Saviour's side?
> Are you washed in the blood of the Lamb?
> Do you rest each moment with the Crucified?
> Are you washed in the blood of the Lamb?

"I realized that when I was running across the country, as outlaw number one, I would have been killed on several occasions if it had not been for His protection."

Floyd recalled that while he and Ted Walters were on their rampage, they once ran into a police ambush in Arkansas.

"We were crossing a small bridge. All of a sudden there were about a dozen officers shooting at us point-blank. The car was drenched with bullet holes. One officer stood only four or five feet away while he shot at me. He missed. It was a miracle.

"I could not doubt that God had put out His protecting hand over me, or that He had something to do with my life. God was also protecting Ted Walters, but Ted never realized that.

"When I got to where I could see that God was protecting me, I said to Him, 'Here's my life. You take it and my affairs and work them out. I can't take care of my life myself. I don't have the power. I don't have the knowledge.'

"I quit telling God how to do it. I just told Him to go ahead and do it—that it was up to Him.

"It seemed then as if a heavy load was lifted from my shoulders.

"I felt really good.

"I knew that everything was going to be alright.

"This was the first time in my life that I felt everything was going to work out right.

"I found I could lay down on my bunk and rest.

"I had peace of mind."

> When the Bridegroom cometh will your robes be white?
> Are you washed in the blood of the Lamb?
> Will your soul be ready for the mansions bright?
> And be washed in the blood of the Lamb?

"You see, up until that time, I thought that if I turned my life over to God I would be releasing all my will to Him, and that I would be forced into doing good, instead of *choosing* to do good. Now my concept of good and evil was altogether different. I found that the things that I wanted to do *were* God's will. He *was* guiding me. He *was* with me."

I reminded Floyd that his experience was a wonderful demonstration of what Jesus said in Matthew 11:28, "Come unto me, all ye that labour and are heavy laden, and I will give you rest."

"That's true," Floyd said, smiling broadly. "It even applies to *Public Enemy Number 1* in a solitary cell in Alcatraz."

After accepting the Lord, Floyd's behavior changed dramatically. He no longer attempted to escape. He continued studying the Bible, and won the respect and admiration of his fellow convicts, the guards, and the warden. He was removed from isolation and allowed to mix freely with the general prison population. Day by day, he grew stronger in the Lord. Floyd had resigned himself to spending the remainder of his life in Alcatraz. But, when he least expected it, he was transferred, because of his good record, back to Leavenworth. From there he went back to Texas prisons for two final years. Then, with the aid of a newspaperman, an auto dealer, and Ted Hinton, one of the officers who had gunned down Bonnie and Clyde, Floyd was released in 1958.

> Lay aside the garments that are stained with sin,
> And be washed in the blood of the Lamb.

There's a fountain flowing for the soul unclean,
O be washed in the blood of the Lamb.

The memory of twenty-two years in prison is seared into
Floyd's mind, though he considers himself fortunate because
there were people who cared about him and were willing to
help. Others aren't as lucky. Therefore, a short time after
becoming a free man, Floyd received a state charter to organize
Con Aid. He turned his home into a halfway house for ex-
convicts. As the former prisoners adjust to freedom, Floyd
supplies them with food, clothing, shelter and Bibles. He also
frequently succeeds in getting them jobs.

"The idea of helping ex-convicts came to me after I accepted Jesus," says Floyd. "It was the Christian way of serving
Him. In prison, I noticed that the young men in particular kept
coming back. It was always the same pattern. A fellow in his
twenties or thirties would get out, but he had no special training to get a job and there wasn't anyone to help him. So he
began associating with his old friends and soon he was back
into his criminal activities and then back in prison."

Floyd also works with young people on the brink of trouble.
Dallas juvenile officers often ask Floyd for help. Not too long
ago, he was asked to use his persuasive powers to talk to a
youngster who worshipped Al Capone.

"The kid had some sort of hang-up about Capone. He even
carried a gun and tried to imitate his hero.

"I told him I knew Capone and that he wasn't the kind of
man anyone would want to be like. The kid's eyes bulged. I
mentioned how Capone wrapped his friends in concrete and
dropped them in a river when he could no longer use them. I
told him that in Alcatraz, Capone wasn't a hero, he was just
another con.

"A couple of days later, the boy's mother called me and said
her son had quit carrying a gun and had gone back to work.
She said he was doing very well."

Floyd has become a crusader for the justice of the Bible. He
says that the revenge and punishment system used in today's
federal and state prisons is obsolete and should be abolished.

He would like to see Attica, Leavenworth, San Quentin and other so-called correctional institutions torn down and replaced with New Life Centers where men and women who run afoul of the law could rebuild their lives and become contributing, tax paying citizens again.

"I'd like each state and the U.S. government to purchase large tracts of land, then build their prisons as model communities or Life Centers so prisoners could learn a trade and earn a living at the same time."

Citing the restitution principle of Scripture, Floyd says those convicted of crimes should pay for what they stole and should pay their own room and board while working in these Centers.

"My plan would do two important things. It would make it possible for a prisoner to support his family while serving his sentence, and it would fit him for a productive, useful life once he's released. I imagine it would phase out the prison system we have now."

So exemplary was Floyd's conduct and readjustment to society that eight years after his parole, President Lyndon Johnson granted him a full pardon in 1966. A year later, Texas Governor John Connally awarded him a state pardon.

Floyd never forgot Ted Walters, his old crime partner who was *Public Enemy Number 2* in the days when he was *Public Enemy Number 1*. Floyd helped secure Walters' release in 1970, appearing personally before the parole board.

Floyd counseled and worked with Walters. But Walters wouldn't accept Floyd's advice—"The Christian way is the only answer to your problems."

Now fifty-eight years old, he was still Terrible Ted. In October 1971 Walters held up a Dallas liquor store with a shotgun. He nearly got away with it. Fleeing the robbery, his car was stopped by a police officer only when he made an illegal right turn. As the officer approached him, Walters began firing his shotgun. The officer returned the fire, wounding him in the shoulder. Walters fled on foot to a nearby house, where he took Mr. and Mrs. Hoyt Houston and their five-year-old daughter as hostages.

Police quickly surrounded the house. Walters emerged with

his three prisoners. He held his shotgun to Mr. Houston's head. Officers stood by helplessly as Walters and his prisoners drove off in the Houston car. But Walters ran into a 150-man police blockade several miles outside town.

The police talked to Walters for twenty minutes. The officers tried to bargain with him. If he would release his hostages unharmed, they would let him drive off. As Walters thought it over, he relaxed, moving his gun away from Mr. Houston's head. A sharpshooting Texas Ranger, Tom Arnold, saw his chance. Fired from a powerful rifle from a distance of one hundred yards, Ranger Arnold's bullet hit Walters in the head. Instantaneously, other officers raced up to the car and fired three more shots into Walters' body. The Houston family was unharmed.

Says Floyd: "The officers tried their best. They tried to convince him to throw down that shotgun and surrender. But Ted said he'd rather be gunned to death like a mad dog than go back to prison. And that's what happened. I don't know what Ted was thinking. He was just mixed up."

Since his release, Floyd has been employed as a night watchman at an Oldsmobile dealership. He doesn't carry a gun. "Even if I had one, I still wouldn't kill a man."

Floyd's been involved in two break-ins. The first time, Floyd called police, who caught a would-be burglar as he fled. The other one Floyd caught himself.

"He was just a teenager and here he was trying to pry open the cashier's window. I talked to him about God, told him a little bit of my life, and let him go. I thought he deserved another chance. I hope he used his second chance wisely."

Floyd is always ready to travel with me to prisons to give his Christian testimony.

One night in 1975, at a crusade I'd organized at the California Men's Colony, Floyd addressed a large congregation in the chapel. Seated in the audience was Tex Watson.

When Floyd finished relating what God had done in his life, something unique happened, something I'd never seen before. All the prisoners rose to their feet spontaneously and gave

Floyd a standing ovation. It was a mark of the respect and admiration they had for him, and a recognition that it takes more courage to live as a Christian than it does to live a life of crime.

For more than two decades now Floyd Hamilton has been able to answer with a resounding YES whenever he sings:

> Have you been to Jesus for the cleansing power?
> Are you washed in the blood of the Lamb?
> Are you fully trusting in His grace this hour?
> Are you washed in the blood of the Lamb?

6

Life for Life

Tragically, murder and violent crime have become as American as apple pie.

No one is safe and there's no place to hide, not in the cities or in the traditionally crime-free small towns of America.

The population of the cattle and farm community of Gordon, Nebraska, is 2,106. In 1972, a helpless alcoholic was murdered near Main Street by four young people ranging in age from eighteen to twenty-seven. Since that killing, more than four hundred felonies, including twenty-two murders, have been committed in the tiny region of Gordon.

There are 3,143,000 people in the San Francisco-Oakland area, America's sixth largest population complex. In 1976, four men were convicted of randomly killing people on the streets of San Francisco. The judge who sentenced them to life imprisonment said the slayings were "vicious, terrifying crimes." Although fourteen persons died of gunfire or stabbing at the hands of the quartet, the defendants were charged directly with only three of the murders. They were also found guilty of four assaults, a rape, and the attempted kidnapping of three children.

According to FBI statistics, in 2,697 cities with a population of under 10,000, the murder rate has increased 28.4 percent since 1970. In the large cities, the increase is 17.8 percent.

Three mathematicians at the Massachusetts Institute of Technology, who made a study of homicide, put the problem in succinct, dramatic perspective: "An American child born in

1976 is more likely to die by murder than an American soldier in World War II was to die in combat."

Dr. Donald T. Lunde, assistant professor of psychiatry and law at Stanford University, who's also made a study of murder, says in equally dramatic terms, "More Americans were homicide victims between 1970 and 1974 than died in the Vietnam War."

Dr. Lunde, one of the psychiatrists who examined Patricia Hearst, declares: "We are experiencing an incredible increase in the murder rate—not only the highest ever recorded in the country but one of the highest in the world." Murders, he says, are approaching an annual rate of one for every 10,000 Americans.

Why?

Dr. Lunde's reasons: Permissive child rearing, government corruption, a decline in self-reliance and an increasing tendency for people to blame their troubles on "society"—not themselves—and thus vent their frustrations by killing other people. The doctor also says that the diminishing influence of religion is an extremely important factor; the loosening of ties to God is in large measure responsible for the surge in murder.

"When traditional values and the Protestant ethic reigned, people felt more responsible for themselves," Dr. Lunde notes. "If they were frustrated, as they were in the Depression when banks were failing, they took it out on themselves and were jumping out of windows."

Organized religion, which taught self-restraint and accountability to God, reaches fewer people today, and government corruption and hypocrisy encourages them to blame others, Dr. Lunde believes. Contrary to popular notion, overall church membership in the United States has been relatively stable since World War II. Some denominations, notably the Southern Baptist Convention, have grown enormously. Southern Baptists comprise the largest Protestant body in America, with 12.5 million members. Forty percent of U.S. adults attend a church or synagogue in an average week, according to the authoritative *1976 Yearbook of American and Canadian Churches.*

Most murders, he points out, are being committed by young adults of the post World War II generation.

"That generation is much more likely to blame others than themselves, because of the way they were reared and because they've grown up in a time when there is much more governmental control. It's much easier to blame the President, or the bureaucracy, or the boss when things go bad.

"I think it may be a good time for parents to reassess their own values and child-rearing practices. I don't think that total permissiveness and strict authoritarianism are the only two approaches to child rearing."

The headlines bear out Dr. Lunde's assertion that murder has become the province of the young—and some who commit homicide are unbelievably young and callous.

A thirteen-year-old girl was sentenced in 1976 for the murder, kidnapping, and robbery of a South San Francisco nurse. She and a nineteen-year-old male companion abducted their victim from a shopping center and forced her into the trunk of her own car. The kidnappers drove for four hours, then opened the trunk and shot their captive in the head. The young killers were caught when crusing policemen spotted the nurse's car they'd stolen on a freeway. The police gave chase at ninety miles per hour.

After their capture, the pair showed little remorse. The nineteen-year-old boy, sentenced to a mere five years in prison, said he'd do it again after he was released! The thirteen-year-old didn't want to murder again, if it could be avoided. The "next time," she said, she would wear a mask to prevent identification by the victim.

Her probation report described her as "sweet and innocent appearing." She "needs a warm, stable, long-term homelike placement." The judge sentenced the girl to parole in a foster home.

In the rush to be lenient to the unrepentant killers, everyone had forgotten about the dead nurse, who had given up her life in a robbery that netted seventeen dollars.

An unpaid twenty-five-dollar debt was sufficient motive for a fifteen-year-old boy in Bakersfield, California, to toss two

Molotov cocktails into the home of a farm worker. Three members of the man's family, including a two-year-old grandson, were burned to death as they slept in the small frame house.

"Violence and other illegal activities by members of youth gangs and groups in the United States of the mid-1970's represent a crime problem of the first magnitude which shows little prospect of early abatement," says Dr. Walter B. Miller of the Harvard Law School's Center for Criminal Justice.

There is also a first-magnitude crime problem at Dr. Miller's doorstep. Though Harvard, located in Cambridge, Massachusetts, spends $1.7 million a year on security, the school is plagued by a variety of crimes ranging from vandalism to murder. In 1975 there were 2,600 crimes reported on the campus. Carol Peterson, a forty-eight-year-old administrative assistant to the dean of the Business School, was stabbed to death in the hallway of her apartment house. Ethel Higonnet, 30, the wife of a professor, was shot to death in the course of a robbery. Says campus director of security David Gorski: "This isn't the Harvard of twenty-five to thirty years ago." He blames most of the crimes on outsiders. "We are in a crime-ridden setting, and we do not have the resources to provide wall-to-wall protection."

Dr. Miller studied gang activities in twelve cities. In some sections of New York, Los Angeles, Philadelphia, Detroit, Chicago and San Francisco, as many as seven out of every hundred youths belonged to a gun-toting gang. He also found serious juvenile gang problems in Cleveland, Washington, St. Louis, Baltimore, New Orleans and Houston.

The most shocking finding of Dr. Miller's study was that there had been 525 gang-related murders in Philadelphia, Los Angeles, Chicago, New York, and San Francisco from 1972 to 1974.

"Murder by firearms or other weapons, the central and most dangerous form of gang-member violence, in all probability stands today at the highest level it has reached in the history of the nation," Dr. Miller says.

He also found that "the schools are a major arena for gang activity. The shooting and killing of teachers by gang members was reported for Chicago and Philadelphia." Gangs have claimed school buildings and surroundings as their territory "to a degree never before reported." Once their territory is established, the gang extorts fees of a quarter to a dollar from students for the "privilege" of passing through hallways or using school facilities.

Dr. Miller says gang members tend to be males between the ages of twelve and twenty-one.

"The prevalence, use, quality and sophistication of weaponry in the gangs of the 1970's far surpass anything known in the past," he adds, citing San Francisco police who listed the cheap handguns known as Saturday night specials as the major gang weapon; however, police in other cities said gangs were armed with high quality weapons, such as the Smith & Wesson .38 caliber revolver.

Another alarming trend in the criminal climate of America is that women are currently committing one out of every four murders!

A New York sociologist, Dr. Florence L. Denmark, and Dr. Ruth Rutschmann-Jaffe of Barnard College, found, after studying the "female crime wave," that there was more behind it than just the women's liberation movement, which is often cited as the cause.

They said: "The female offender, whether acting by herself or with others, is not typically the emancipated intellectual striving for civil liberties.

"Her crime is rarely an assertion of equal rights, or an unconscious attempt at achieving her own or others' rights."

The doctors said that the rate of increase in female arrests since 1960 was three times that of males. Female arrests for violent crimes increased by 278 percent compared to 88 percent for men.

"Clearly, women are no longer limiting themselves to so-called traditionally female crimes of shoplifting and prostitution. Kitchen knives have given way to pistols and sawed-off shotguns."

The doctors couldn't precisely pin down the reasons for the upsurge in female crime. They said the explanation probably involved an interaction of religious, psychological, social, economic and political factors.

The FBI confirms that criminal activities by women have increased in every category. Not only are women committing 25% of the nation's murders, but the rate of increase in female arrests since 1960 is up for aggravated assault by 10%; burglary, 14%; arson, 28.7%; embezzlement, 37.5%, and driving under the influence of drugs or alcohol 47%.

Los Angeles Deputy District Attorney Aaron Stovitz feels that juries are more lenient toward women defendants than toward men.

"I can point to a dozen cases of women killing their spouses and the jury acquitting them. And to another dozen where the woman was convicted of manslaughter—a conviction which was reversed on appeal—and then acquitted on retrial.

"Some juries reason that [in killing her husband] she would not kill again. If she were found guilty and imprisoned for the crime the state would have to take care of her children."

He recalls a woman whose husband was murdered in his sleep. The first jury could not reach a verdict and the second acquitted her on grounds of self-defense!

Another woman and her gardener were charged with killing her husband. The gardener was let off on an insanity plea and the jury then acquitted the wife.

"It's amazing," Stovitz said, "how lenient juries can be."

Los Angeles municipal court judge Leila Bulgrin looks at her female contemporaries and shakes her head sadly. She thinks a more permissive society and the more frequent use of drugs should both be blamed for the growing numbers of women in crime.

"You once could assume that a woman in crime was only a follower and was simply surviving when she was mixed up in a criminal situation. But you cannot assume this at all any more. The girls are initiating the destructive activity. Some of them come into court looking as hard as nails. They are jaded and tough.

"I never used to see girls like this ten years ago. I think children cannot stand the enormous amount of freedom they are given. Maybe I'm old-fashioned, but I think girls are not protected enough by their families.

"Parents sometimes take it easy with discipline in the early years which causes tragedy later when the youngster is brought to court as a juvenile or adult offender."

Police officer Linda Monahan, who works in a Los Angeles women's jail, says that drug-addicted and alcoholic women are the most difficult to handle.

"Women use dirtier language than men when they are angry," Officer Monahan says.

"There is little to do in the cells and we put the women together so they can talk. There are phone calls, showers, breakfast, dinner, and visits with investigators and that's about all you can do."

Perhaps the most frightening aspect of crime is the rise of the mass killer. The San Francisco case in which fourteen were murdered helter-skelter is but one example.

In 1958, Charles Raymond Starkweather and his fourteen-year-old girl friend Caril Ann Fugate murdered ten people. The pair were caught, charged, tried and convicted. Miss Fugate, because she was a minor, was sentenced to life. She was paroled in 1976, after serving eighteen years. Starkweather, nineteen, "rode the lightning." The death penalty had not yet been outlawed and, as the recipient of swift justice, he was executed in the electric chair at the Nebraska State Penitentiary in June 1959.

Says writer William Allen: The Starkweather-Fugate murders "marked the beginning of a trend toward increased violence on the part of individuals acting in relative autonomy in this country."

The next mass murder rampage to horrify Americans was the butchery in 1966 of eight student nurses by a onetime garbageman and apprentice seaman named Richard Speck.

When he was trapped in a Chicago flophouse, he attempted to commit suicide. Thwarted, he stood trial, and the jury sentenced him to 1,200 years.

On one of my visits to Joliet, I met Speck. He's a tall, thin thirty-five-year-old man with blue eyes and blond hair. On his left forearm is a tattoo that reads: "Born to Raise Hell."

"I didn't kill those eight nurses," was the first thing Richard Speck said to me. "I had witnesses who were ready to testify that I was in another city when those murders took place. They wouldn't let my witnesses testify that I couldn't have done it."

I didn't argue the point with him. That isn't what I was there for. I was there to tell him that God loves sinners, that there is mercy through Jesus Christ.

I learned that after I left, Speck went to the chaplain and asked, "What did Chaplain Ray want with me? Why did he really want to see me?"

The chaplain replied, "For no other reason than to tell you about Jesus."

The chaplain told me he was greatly encouraged by Speck's visit. Up to that time he had never before been in his office.

I can't say at this moment that Richard Speck has become a Christian or that he's changed his story. I can say he's heard the good news that God loves prisoners.

I never give up on anyone. I plan to see Richard Speck again, and, hopefully, become the vessel through which he comes to the Lord. ". . . for I am not come to call the righteous, but sinners to repentance," says Jesus in Matthew 9:13.

The litany of multiple murder seems never ending:

—Juan Corona, thirty-eight, was sentenced to life in January 1973 for the brutal slaying of twenty-five itinerant farm workers in Yuba City, California.

—In Houston, Texas, thirty-three-year-old Dean Coryl tortured and murdered at least thirty young men until he himself was killed in 1973 by Elmer Henley, his seventeen-year-old accomplice.

—From December 1, 1974, until January 29, 1975, the Skid Row quarter of Los Angeles was plagued by a Slasher who had cut the throats of nine men. The alleged killer had been paroled after serving nine years for two 1964 murders. In his new round of crime, the Slasher case wasn't all. The purported murderer was given a sentence of thirty-two years to life for a series of crimes that included a hatchet attack on two men and the burglary of actor Burt Reynolds' hillside home in Hollywood.

—In May 1976, David McRae, Jr., twenty-two, walked into a bar in a seedy area of Norfolk, Virginia, and, without warning, fatally shot four people. He then turned the gun on himself and took his own life. As a teenager, McRae had been a police cadet. His ambition was to become a professional policeman. His tragic mistake was to assume he could be judge, jury and executioner. The bar had a reputation as a hangout for pimps, prostitutes and dope pushers, and McRae, in his mother's words, "didn't like for people to do anything wrong." Carter L. Wilson, the former director of the Police Community Relations Division who knew McRae when he was a cadet, said: "He was eager to do something worthwhile and had a great deal of frustration as a result of not being able to do anything he felt was of real value." He added that McRae was interested in the "elimination of crime."

This catalogue of corrosive mass murder seems likely to continue until the hearts of men are moved by God.

Newspapers, magazines and television bombard us daily with virtually the same horrendous story. In Ventura, California: TRIAL SET FOR MAN IN SLAYING OF FOUR. In Indianapolis, Indiana: KILLER MURDERS SEVEN. In Baltimore, Maryland: CRAZED MAN KILLS COUNCILMAN, THREE OTHERS IN GUN BATTLE. In Boston: SLAYER OF EIGHT STILL AT LARGE. On a Los Angeles television station: "A berserk killer wantonly murdered five people today." *Psychology Today* magazine offers us a "Portrait of a Mass Killer."

The most popular solution for murder and violent crime is money. But if money could have done the job, America would be the Garden of Eden.

In 1969, Congress passed the Omnibus Crime Control and Safe Streets Act.

A staggering $4.4 billion was disbursed to U.S. cities to reduce murder and other crime.

What happened?

"The nation is in no better position today than it was when the Act was initiated," said a 1976 report of the independent, objective Center for National Security Studies. "Crime has increased and no solutions to the crime problems are on the horizon."

The Center criticized the government for its well-meaning program "which had no clear objective and preconceived idea of what would work."

The Center's report ended with these words: "The federal government has greatly increased its expenditures to combat crime, but these expenditures have had no effect in reducing crime. It is the conclusion of this report that the government's program should be abolished."

Instead of foregoing the program, which the Center accurately said hadn't worked, Congress appropriated another massive infusion of money to fund the Crime Control Act—this time the bill would be $5 billion for a program doomed to failure.

Imagine the impact in this country if there was $5 billion available for soul-winning Christians to revamp the prison system according to laws of Scripture. The thought boggles the mind.

Any discussion of murder inevitably leads to a dialogue concerning the death penalty—a subject the Bible deals with unequivocally.

"Whoso sheddeth man's blood, by man shall his blood be shed," Genesis 9:6 asserts.

The Sixth Commandment—Exodus 21:13—declares in four unambiguous words: "Thou shalt not kill."

Several verses later, in Exodus 21:22–25, the Scripture makes itself equally clear: ". . . he shall pay as the judges determine . . . life for life. Eye for eye, tooth for tooth, hand for hand, foot for foot, Burning for burning, wound for wound, stripe for stripe."

Jesus said in Matthew 19:18: ". . . Thou shalt not do murder."

". . . the wages of sin is death . . ." adds Romans 6:23.

Thus, God's word concerning the death penalty is clear.

My close friend, Dr. Stewart McBirnie, senior pastor of the United Community Church in Glendale, California, and one of the nation's finest, most adroit theologians, says:

"God was the first to practice the death penalty. The flood

of Noah's day was God's method of capital punishment.

"Nowhere in the Bible does Jesus abrogate the responsibility of the State to punish murder. He even submitted Himself to the death sentence that was imposed upon Him by a Roman court. Two other prisoners were executed beside Him the day he died. He did nothing to prevent their execution. But the prisoner who confessed his faith in Jesus and who also confessed that he deserved the death penalty for his crimes, was given something far better than a mere extension of his human life. He was given the promise, 'Thou shalt be with me in Paradise.' "

In 1972 the Supreme Court of the U.S. ruled in a close decision (5 to 4) that the death penalty as then applied was unconstitutional.

Since then, however, thirty-five states have passed laws restoring capital punishment. They endeavored to conform their state laws to the guidelines indicated by the decision of the Supreme Court.

In every state where the voters have been given an opportunity to express their views by their ballots the death penalty has been restored.

Most voters are of the opinion that we have had the death penalty in force all along. But to the voters it appears that the penalty was paid only by the victims, and that the killers acted as arresting officer, prosecutor, judge, jury, and executioner. There was no appeal for the victim. This made human life too cheap, allowing a criminal to take a human life without forfeiting his own.

A life for a life is simply evenhanded justice. Nevertheless, it makes no provision for restituion, for a killer cannot restore the life that he has taken.

The argument of whether or not the death penalty is a deterrent to killings cannot be proven from past experience in the United States. At no time in our history was it a certainty that anyone and everyone guilty of first-degree murder would be executed. Only a very small percentage of murderers have paid with their lives for their crimes. At times there was remote possibility that a murderer would have to pay with his life, but this is not a true deterrent.

A significant 1976 Gallup poll showed that a whopping 65 percent of Americans support the death penalty for murder, reflecting the average citizen's stomach-churning fear and disgust concerning the magnification of the homicide rate.

For more than a decade, Dr. George Gallup and his pollsters have asked a representative sample of Americans the same question: "Are you in favor of the death penalty for persons convicted of murder?"

Note the dramatic shift in opinion since 1966 in the following Gallup table:

Year	Yes	No	No Opinion
1976	65%	28%	7%
1972	57%	32%	11%
1969	51%	40%	9%
1966	42%	47%	11%

The recent 7–2 decision of the Surpreme Court, restoring the death penalty within the guidelines set by the court, reflects quite accurately the sentiments of the voters of this nation.

Citing FBI statistics that showed a 50 percent jump in the homicide rate in a five-year period, Justice Lewis F. Powell, Jr. said in 1976: "It is perfectly obvious from these figures that we need some way to deter the slaughter of Americans." Justice Harry A. Blackmun chided foes of the death penalty for ignoring the "innocent victims" of murderers. Chief Justice Warren E. Burger and Justice William H. Rehnquist made similar remarks in support of capital punishment.

As a Bible believer, I recognize and accept the principle of "life for life." I abhor the idea that a man has the right to take another man's life and still retain his own.

But it takes a disciplined, moral nation with strong convictions to exercise the death penalty and mete it out fairly and quickly.

Stanford's Dr. Lunde says: "Whatever its legal status, the

death penalty has been actually administered in less than half of 1 percent of murder cases in modern times."

Dr. McBirnie cites the fact that the courtroom too often is an arena where only the poor receive punishment. But he adds: "The cure lies not in abolishing the death penalty, but in seeing to it that court reform changes the procedures of law so that none can escape its justice. It is jurisprudence with its endless delays, loopholes, the possibility of interminable appeals, which is to blame for the inequities between rich and poor."

I would favor the death penalty only if the entire system of justice were overhauled. If the system worked so that *every* person, no matter his wealth or position, knew that when the commits first-degree murder that within ninety days of apprehension and trial he would be executed, thousands of lives would be saved.

That's why the Founding Fathers said in the sixth amendment to the Bill of Rights that "the accused shall enjoy the right to a speedy and public trial."

Solomon speaks to the same point in Ecclesiastes 8:11: "Because sentence against an evil work is not executed speedily, therefore the heart of the sons of men is fully set in them to do evil."

Historically, quick, early justice has always reduced crime. As our system works now, if one hundred crimes are committed, no more than twenty arrests will be made. Of those twenty arrested, no more than three will be sent to prison. Which means that the crime business, statistically, is fairly lucrative and the risk of arrest and punishment is fairly small. But if those figures were reversed and all one hundred criminals were speedily convicted and punished, the crime rate would drop precipitously.

The same equation should hold true in the case of murder and the death penalty. In biblical Israel, the death penalty was administered rapidly and equitably. Rich and poor were treated exactly alike. In our present-day adversary system of justice, the poor and members of minorities have borne the brunt of capital punishment.

Why is it that in our system money "talks"? A poor man, as so often happens, is convicted because he cannot afford to hire an adroit attorney. He usually must content himself with a busy, overworked public defender who does not have time to prepare his defense adequately. The poor man may be convicted although the prosecutor has a weak case.

On the other hand, a wealthy man, able to afford a clever lawyer, is more often than not set free even if the prosecutor has a strong case.

Seldom has a rich man received the maximum sentence. When Richard Loeb and Nathan Leopold kidnapped and murdered fourteen-year-old Bobby Franks in 1924, the case was the sensation of its day. Public opinion overwhelmingly demanded that Loeb and Leopold should pay with their lives. Their wealthy fathers hired Clarence Darrow, a spellbinding lawyer, and paid him one million dollars to save their sons from the death penalty. Darrow was successful. Loeb and Leopold were sentenced to life plus ninety-nine years. Loeb was killed in a prison fight by a fellow inmate in 1936. Leopold's "life plus ninety-nine years" sentence ended in 1958 with his parole. He died in a villa in Puerto Rico in 1971.

Not much has changed since 1924. Only the rich can afford to hire silver-tongued attorneys. Jesus said in Luke 11:46: ". . . . Woe unto you also, ye lawyers! for ye lade men with burdens grievous to be borne. . . ."

Grievous burdens will continue to plague our system of justice—and the point bears repeating—until lawyers, judges, penologists and prisoners learn that the only cure for crime is God and His law.

That lesson was learned by one of the nation's most cold-blooded killers, who, it seemed, couldn't be reached by God. Yet. . . .

7

Murf the Surf

The *Star of India*, a 563.35-carat sapphire, glistened in the reflected light of two small overhead bulbs.

Almost as large as a golf ball, the precious jewel from the collection of the fabled financier J.P. Morgan was enclosed in a glass case at New York's Museum of Natural History. The stone was considered burglar-proof. Every possible precaution had been taken to avoid its theft.

But on the roof of the public parking lot adjacent to the museum, Jack Roland Murphy, a twenty-nine-year-old Miami Beach playboy, and a confederate were nevertheless preparing to steal the *Star*. Another accomplice, with a walkie-talkie, remained outside the building as a lookout.

It was October 29, 1964, and the night was iron cold. Murf and his helper were dressed in warm, dark clothing as they used a climbing rope to lower themselves thirty feet from the roof of the parking lot to the museum's courtyard.

The *Star* reposed on the fifth floor, seemingly a mile away. But the challenge wasn't beyond the acrobatic talents of Murf the Surf. He and his pals had cased and rehearsed the heist for weeks. A few nights before, Murf had hosted a party at his penthouse. Bragging to a girl that he had the dexterity of a cat burglar, he said he could easily lower himself from his terrace to the terrace of the tenant below. Using only his hands, he hung suspended for a long moment three hundred feet in the air until he safely completed the dangerous stunt.

Now Murf was faced with a far more difficult challenge. He

started up the wall of the museum building in human-fly fashion, clutching at crevices and pieces of decorative stone. He moved with tantalizing but efficient slowness, inch by inch, until he finally reached the coping extending from the fifth floor. Hanging by his fingers, he swung his body into the gem room through the window. He'd made it.

Murf scooped up twenty-four precious stones, including *the Star* and the 100-carat De Long ruby. Their value at the time was $410 thousand. Today they would easily bring more than $2 million.

With their loot, the trio took the first flight back to Miami Beach. But they were arrested forty-eight hours after the job, before they could fence the stones, by New York detectives, who had caught them, thanks to an anonymous tip. (Someone has rightly said, "Whenever man commits a crime heaven finds a witness.")

Murf and his confreres were extradited, and on February 8, 1965, they all pleaded guilty to grand larceny, burglary and possession of burglar tools.

The judge said: "The very nature of the crime, when examined in the light of the background of these defendants, does little to commend any one of them for favorable or sympathetic consideration.

"However, I am more than satisfied that by the return of these jewels the community has been immeasurably enriched."

The judge then sentenced the trio to three years each.

It wasn't the first time that Jack Roland Murphy had been in trouble with the law. He'd been arrested several times from New York to California for robbery and fraud.

"I grew up out West," Murf told me a number of years later when I interviewed him at the Florida State Prison. "I was born and raised in California, but my father was a lineman and we traveled extensively."

Murf said that as a youngster he'd been in Oregon, Washington, New Mexico and Idaho while his father helped string high power lines across that part of the United States.

Despite the rootlessness, Murf remembers his childhood as ideal.

"It was a wonderful environment. My parents and their friends were patriotic Americans and God-fearing people. I never heard a word of prejudice uttered about any member of a minority. It was nothing unusual for me as a child to play with Mexican, black or Indian friends."

The influence of God was always strong within the Murphy family.

"I have several aunts who live in Albuquerque, New Mexico, who have been missionaries on Indian reservations and in Mexican communities who've just been giants for the Lord for over forty years. They shared the Lord with me all my life.

"My parents were good people who constantly promoted church to me. As a child I went to church. I went to this church, that church, and in moving as much as I did I was constantly in different kinds of churches. So church is nothing new to me. I was aware of religion, aware of people reaching up for God. I knew what a Christian atmosphere was. As a youngster, I played the violin and I played in churches all the time."

Murf's trouble, of course, was that he'd never had a born-again experience with Jesus, despite all the churches he attended.

When Murf was a teenager, his family settled in McKeesport, Pennsylvania. There he attended high school and then went to the University of Pennsylvania, but dropped out without graduating. That was a particular shame in Murf's case. He was eminently suited to enter one of the professions. His IQ is 126, a distinction shared only by about one in five Americans.

When he left the University, Murf succumbed to the lure of Miami Beach. He'd read that it was America's Sodom. And Sodom is where he wanted to be.

"I don't think I could have gone to a worse place, because that city is really immature spiritually," Murf now reflects.

"I looked around and saw tourists down there just partying and having a fantastic time. So I figured that if it's good enough for these people who come once every few years to party, I'm going to be here all the time and party all the time."

Murf admired the people he met. "They had money. They had success. They must be correct in what they are doing and the way they are living."

He said he got caught up in the all-American pastime of chasing the dollar. And that eventually led to crime. He envied "everyone with a big car and the women in mink coats" whom he saw at the racetracks and in the posh hotels.

At first he worked for a living. He was a beachboy for a time, earning three dollars a day plus tips. Then came stints as a tennis pro, a dance instructor, a swimming teacher, and a real estate salesman. But Murf wanted more excitement. He became a high-tower acrobatic diver, and traveled throughout the country with the Barnum & Bailey and Shrine circuses. Finally, he returned to Miami Beach and went into the surfing business. The surfboards he manufactured and offered for sale led to his "Murf the Surf" cognomen when he became a criminal celebrity.

"Was it a happy life?" I asked Murf.

"I liked riding the waves," he said. "There is a sort of communion with God when you're in the ocean. There's a peacefulness out there at times. I was away from people, away from society, away from the materialistic chase after pleasure, and I was with nature. I've always enjoyed the outdoors. I enjoyed being out with the birds, and the waves, and the beach, and the serenity and peacefulness that's out there.

"The rest of it was nothing. I was constantly chasing, constantly having to go outside myself for my happiness. I would get up in the morning and think, Wow, I'm going to get a six-pack of beer. I'm going down to the beach and find a chick. I'm going to go someplace and get some of this happiness. If only I could buy that big car, I would be happy."

Murf said he got into crime as "an adventure, an escape, another avenue of pursuing pleasure." Thanks to several lucrative thefts, Murf soon had all the outer trappings of success.

"I had money. I had cars. I was married several times. The atmosphere in Miami Beach was like having your own harem. You'd walk into a hotel or stroll on the beach and there'd be two hundred girls for every man.

"But no matter where I went, I could not find that happiness, that peace. There was a great void in my life. I looked around and saw that other people had that void in their lives, too."

This would have been an appropriate time for Murf to have concentrated on his surfing business. It could have been profitable, but Murf never explored its full potential. It would also have been an appropriate time for Murf to seek the lasting peace of God, heeding the advice of James 4:2: ". . . ye have not, because ye ask not."

Instead he chose to continue his career in crime, most notably the *Star of India* burglary. He returned to Miami Beach after serving his sentence and returned, also, to a hedonistic life.

"I had to come to the belly of hell to find peace, to find Jesus Christ," Murf told me. Murf is a talented painter. In one of his canvases, he depicts the Florida State Prison as existing inside the belly of a whale. He calls the painting *The Belly of Hell*. His passport to the prison was murder.

A pair of secretaries, Terry Rae Kent Frank, twenty-three, and Annelle Mohn, twenty-one, came to Miami Beach with $488 thousand in negotiable securities which they'd stolen from a brokerage house where they worked.

The secretaries met Murf and told him about their theft. Murf said he could cash the securities, and the girls gave him the valuable paper.

One night in December 1967, the body of Miss Frank was found in Whisky Creek, near Hollywood, Florida. The body of Miss Mohn was never recovered.

Another anonymous tip led to Murf's arrest. He was tried for the murder.

During the trial, psychiatrist Mordecai Haber, testifying for the defense, said, "Murf has an antisocial personality with sociopathic behavior. His pursuits are hedonistic. He satisfies his own needs. He is aware of customs, rules, and the mores of society, but he has no regard for them."

The angry prosecutor, Ed Stephany, declared: "Terry Kent Frank died as no human being on this earth should die—she was beaten on the head and her stomach was ripped open."

Even Murf's attorney, Jack Nageley, didn't have a good

word to say about his client. After the trial, Nageley said: "He's the worst criminal in the world. I know criminals—some of the best. They have a saying, 'No self-respecting criminal would have anything to do with Murphy.' "

While the jury pondered his fate, Murf, apparently unconcerned, calmly read *Thoughts and Meditations* by poet-mystic Kahlil Gibran. Murf underlined one passage: "An honest man is reviled while liars and immoral men are rewarded with possessions."

But there was to be no reward for Murf. He was convicted and given two life terms plus twenty years, plus two additional terms of five years. Short of the death penalty, it was the harshest sentence that Floridians could remember in any criminal case.

Miami Daily News' reporters Milt Sosin and Jack Mann said Murf was "convicted, and sentenced to life in prison for the cruel, grisly murder of a young girl who, somehow, stood between Jack Murphy and the fabulous spoils he would exact from a society that didn't deserve them. It was a wicked, unfair world that had to be resisted, defeated and punished."

Bitter, fear parading inside him like a strutting drum majorette, Murf entered Florida State Prison as convict number A024627.

"When a man first comes to prison there is a period of fright, then introspection," Murf said, recalling his feelings during his first year behind the walls. "You lay back in your cell, and you wonder, What's it all about? Why am I in this predicament? What's the answer to the mystery of life and death?"

Murf said that every time he was in jail, he received letters from Hawaii, Mexico, Canada, and Washington.

"These were letters from Christians. I didn't get letters from the bartenders, the hoodlums, and all the wise guys that I hung around with. I got letters from Christians whom I didn't even know. They were telling me about Christ. They were telling me that Jesus loves me. Soon my cell was filled with letters and tracts.

"I resisted the Lord at first. Many times I took those letters and just scanned through and ignored them."

61941

But the tendrils of childhood religion were restirred. A huge grin suddenly suffuses Murf's aquiline features as he remembers.

"Chaplain Ray, deep inside I always knew there was something more in the universe, something that wasn't man-made.

"I began reading those letters from witnessing Christians, and I felt good, felt even better than I did when I rode the surf.

"I went to the prison's Bible class. Then I let Jesus come into my life.

"My complete acceptance of Jesus wasn't an immediate thing. It didn't happen overnight. It wasn't a thing where I came into the prison chapel one day and the Holy Spirit just shook me, and grabbed me, and threw me down on the altar, and I just glowed while sirens went off and bells rang.

"It wasn't anything like that. God came to me gradually but when He came, He came to stay!"

Murf said the Bible verse that influenced him most profoundly was Matthew 25:36 in which Jesus says: "Naked, and ye clothed me: I was sick and ye visited me: I was in prison and ye came unto me."

Murf's oneness with the Lord was also aided by the prison chaplain, Reverend Max Jones, and repeated visits from Reverend Gary Horton, of Teen Challenge, and Reverend R.B. Thieme, of Houston, Texas. "They spoke my language and communicated with me in a way I could understand. They taught me to stand tall, to realize that accepting Jesus was a man's game. Another man who helped was ex-gangster Frank Costantino, who'd been converted in prison years before. I'd known Frank for years and he came in here and radiated truth to me."

The smile lingers on Murf's face. "Even now, after ten years in prison, the only people who continually visit me are Christians like yourself. The only people who write me are people like you. The only people who give me courage and constantly reinforce my faith are people like Chaplain Ray and your sisters and brothers in Christ."

Jack Roland Murphy, whose life was once squeezed between a rock and a hard place, is no longer bitter or resentful.

"Now I'm a responsible person. I don't say, as I once did, that the police put me in here; that the judge put me in here. *I* put myself in here. But I'm coping with my problems and handling them with the help of the Lord.

"I praise God for all He has done for me, and for the wonderful work He's accomplished in the lives of some of my friends here. I feel quite compassionate toward the prisoners here who aren't able to understand Jesus. They just sit and stare at the blank walls, and seethe futilely inside. They are just void of answers. But if they'd come to Jesus as I did, He would make all the difference in their lives.

"Those who've cried out to Christ for forgiveness and mercy and life everlasting have been transformed from callous shells into men who stand eight feet tall for the Lord.

"Like me, they glow with the wonderful love of Jesus Christ, and their lives have a new direction. Even here in prison their lives are vital.

"Coming to Christ is an adventure they never found behind a gun, or in a fast automobile, or behind a bar.

"Now they're walking in the love and the light of the Lord, and they are beautiful people. I just praise God for doing that around me, where I can see it and just share in that wonderful, wonderful grace that the Lord has for all of us."

How does Murf confront a future in which he may spend the rest of his life in prison?

"I have many things I want to do on the outside. I'd like to return to the free world. But if it isn't God's will, that's fine with me.

"Being in prison isn't that big a burden anymore, because the Lord is with me. He's serving my time with me in my cell. That's all the strength I need to face the future."

8

The Perry Mason of Florida

It was the bleakest day in Gene Neill's life, this Tuesday in November 1971. In the company of three guards, Gene, a handsome man with a firm jaw, and salt and pepper hair, was walking the dank tunnel under the federal prison at Springfield, Missouri. In a moment they were going to lock him up and throw away the key. It had all happened so quickly. Only a few months before, he'd been one of the richest, most successful lawyers in the nation—at the zenith of his influence and power.

The guards stopped at an eyelet of a cell. One said, "Get in, big shot." When Gene hesitated, he was pushed inside. With a chill laugh, the unfriendly guard said, "We'll be back for you in fifty years!"

Springfield! Gene would come to know the prison well. The government's maximum security institution had taken the place of Alcatraz as the home of the nation's most unredeemable prisoners. Convicts with severe emotional problems were sent here. Prisoners with no hope of parole were sent here. In the cell to the left of Gene was a wizened American Indian who was still serving time for robbing a stagecoach! And Springfield was where the *Birdman of Alcatraz* had died.

Gene was stunned. He tried to think, think about where he was and where he'd been. His thoughts were sundered by screams from other inmates in the cellblock. Later, when I met Gene, he would explain: "Those men weren't screaming from pain, it was just the anguish of being locked in Springfield for so many years. It was a pathetic place."

Fifty years! How, Gene wondered, does a man face that long a sentence? He was forty years old, and convinced he'd never be paroled. Forty wasted years old. My God, he thought, he'd be ninety when he was released. His son, who was three, would be fifty-three years of age.

Gene examined his cell. A pillow, a blanket, a cot. It was so small he could stretch his hands and come within a few inches of touching both walls.

He felt like screaming, too. Worse, he wished he could die. He had reached the nadir of his life—hopeless—no future. He wouldn't live till ninety—he'd die in this cell. He was buried alive. When the guard had slammed his cell door, it was as if a lid had been placed on his coffin.

Gene hadn't been permitted shoes, socks, underwear, or a belt. Only a denim shirt and a size 50 pair of pants, so large he had to hold them up with his hands.

He stripped naked. Possessed by a force he didn't understand, he got down on his knees and prayed, which was an extremely unusual thing for him to do.

Gene Neill was an atheist. . . .

"I think the whole key to what happened to me is that I was raised in a very wealthy neighborhood in Coral Gables, Florida."

Without flinching, without holding anything back, Gene was telling me the story of his incredible life for my nationwide broadcasts.

"I went to church when I was young but I just never saw God there. In the church I went to, they never talked about Jesus. They talked about building campaigns, expansion programs, and money. But nobody talked about Jesus."

Gene grew up feeling that God didn't exist. His studies at the University of Miami did nothing to change that belief. He took courses in philosophy, and soon he was calling himself an *ethical hedonist,* which, says Gene, "means that I thought there's no such thing as morality. If you saw something you wanted, you took it. If something felt good, you did it."

Gene watched a great deal of television. His favorite program was *Perry Mason*. He decided he'd emulate his television hero and become a criminal attorney.

"I thought it would be great if I could have that much power. Power meant money. Though I'd been raised in an affluent family, having my own money, I was certain, would give me the peace I'd been searching for. After all, what else was there in life except money?

"So I got into the criminal law thing strictly to get as much out of it as I could. My ideals certainly weren't as pure as Perry Mason's. I'd win as many cases as possible, but not on behalf of the clients I'd represent and certainly not in the name of justice. I'd win the cases for Gene Neill and his reputation—for Gene Neill's ego and the passport to the good life I was accustomed to."

As often as possible, Gene went to the criminal courts building on Miami's Flagler Street.

"Suddenly I found myself hanging around there. Watching. And learning. And what an incredible melodrama I saw—a moving monolith of emotions, triumph, tragedy, depravity and exhilaration. A staggering tableau of human frailty and victory. Life in its most raw and naked state, where the criminal lawyer is a god. And I wanted to be a god."

Gene went to law school, breezed through the three-day bar exam, and received his doctorate in Jurisprudence cum laude in 1961.

He joined a law firm, and was soon on the road to wealth and fame. He was winning case after case, commanding higher and higher fees. He was married, and had two children, his son, Cole, and daughter, Lydia. Gene bought an expensive home, expensive car and an ocean racing-class sloop.

"I really started getting like old King Midas. Everything I touched seemed to turn to gold, and I thought I was just about the biggest shot ever to come down the pike."

But there was a snake of unhappiness in Gene's "Garden of Eden."

"I became overbearing, intolerable, and insufferable at home. I nagged, demanded, and abused, I guess because at the office I was always driving, and grasping, and climbing. I was a successful lawyer but I was frustrated."

As Gene's practice increased, he saw less and less of his children and his wife, Beverly.

Meanwhile, more storm clouds were gathering.

Gene quit his law firm after a dispute with one of the partners that turned the air blue with obscenities and recriminations. Gene accused the partner of cheating him out of twenty thousand dollars. In Gene's scale of values, losing money was the ultimate sin. When he got no satisfaction, Gene walked out.

The incident that would lead to the end of his marriage began with a frightening phone call.

"Gene, this is Beverly. I've been arrested and I'm in jail. Can you get me out?"

By the time Gene got to the jail, his wife had been booked, mugged and fingerprinted. The charge was shoplifting. Gene put up her bail. In the trial that took place a few weeks later Gene learned, according to the psychiatric report, that *he* was responsible for Beverly's shoplifting.

Fingering the report, the judge said: "Your wife wanted to be caught, because of her unfortunate marriage. It was a way of getting your attention. And this isn't the first time she's shoplifted. She's been doing it for some time now and has been returning the stolen items for money refunds. And you have a charge account at that store and several thousand dollars in your checking account.

"Based on this psychiatric report, I am going to withhold adjudication and sentence, and give you an opportunity to rehabilitate her. But you are going to have to really do something right now, or she'll be back here soon."

Gene never got a chance to rehabilitate his wife. A short time later, they were divorced, and Gene, who was lonely and more empty than ever, was remarried, to a vivacious redheaded legal secretary named Dorothy, who would suffer deeply with him until Gene began living for the Lord.

Gene's next job was as a public defender in Dade County. It paid less than private practice, but Gene felt it would be good for his career and for his "Perry Mason" image.

In the first year he handled two hundred and fifty cases and won 85 percent of them. "That's a higher win score than most criminal lawyers attain in a lifetime of practice," Gene says.

Gene's most dazzling case involved a prisoner who had been in the Florida State Penitentiary for thirty years for robbing a man of eight cents! And he still had to spend the rest of his life there according to his sentence. Life for eight cents! The worst part of it, Gene says, was that the judge who'd given him that incredibly unfair sentence was later disbarred. And a few years afterwards, the prosecutor on the case did time in the Atlanta Federal Prison for violation of the White Slave Act.

Gene had the prisoner's conviction set aside and he was released.

After that case and several others which also were headline grabbers, the newspapers indeed began calling Gene "The Perry Mason of Florida."

Gene soon got fed up with his public defender's job, laid low by "the incredible corruption" he saw among judges, cops, prosecutors, court reporters, bailiffs, and clerks. "They bought and sold cases as though they were commodities. A drunk-driving case could be dismissed for a couple of hundred dollars. A misdemeanor for five hundred. Felonies came higher. A clerk could lose a file or an important pleading, or a reporter could change the transcript. Just a word here or a word there could throw a case. Cops could forget the facts or the faces, or be sick at home on the day of trial. And a prosecutor could 'accidentally' confuse subpoenas so the witnesses weren't there, or 'accidentally' fail to prove the chain of evidence that would lead to a conviction in, say, a big dope case."

Rather than return to private practice, Gene decided a sojourn with the Special Prosecution Division of the State Attorney's Office would be valuable.

He was accepted immediately and given a very important case, the Harbor Island Spa robbery trial. It was the biggest robbery in the history of the state of Florida. The police said that $8 million had been stolen from the resort.

The defendants were Tulio Costerelli, Genero Gaultieri and John Matera.

Gene put dozens of witnesses on the stand, including one

man who said he'd overheard the trio planning the heist.

Costerelli received a directed verdict of not guilty. But Gaultieri got thirty-five years and Matera life.

"And now I was really a big shot! My name had been in all the papers for weeks, and the television cameras were always looking for me as I came out of the courtroom. I really thought I was *something!*

"I kept patting myself on the back. I wasn't just one of forty run-of-the-mill staff prosecutors, I was one of the three specially picked and seasoned trial lawyers who tried all the really heavy cases. And all the cases I prosecuted were big publicity cases—well-known hoods of the underworld. Organized crime figures. Mafia!

"Big shot Gene Neill."

By now Gene and Dorothy had a three-year-old daughter, Heather. They also had a huge plush floating home on the Miami River. It was a large and luxurious two-story houseboat with walnut paneling, a spiral staircase, thick wall-to-wall shag carpeting, stained glass windows, sun porches, and a cedar shake Bermuda roof. It was stocked with gallons of liquor. Dockside, Gene had another new car, a Lincoln Continental.

Gene hosted stag parties on the houseboat. A friend from the county clerk's office would bring reels of confiscated pornographic movies from the evidence room of the criminal court and show them to Gene's guests, which included judges, prosecutors, public defenders, doctors, lawyers and newspaper reporters. Nobody seemed to think it odd that there were also a number of underworld hoodlums who attended these affairs. The parties were reprehensible enough but, even worse, the law and the lawless fraternized easily together, and were members of the same chummy club.

Soon Gene was out hunting bigger game. He returned to private practice, joining a prestigious law firm, and a yacht club, country club, and an international financier set of elite lawyers.

"Within a few years," says Gene, "I was one of the very best criminal lawyers in Miami. Perhaps in the South. Maybe in the country. I had a fancy suite of offices and was making more money than I could spend."

Clients were waiting in line for Gene's services. Many of the big Mafia figures he'd prosecuted as a state attorney came to him to represent them on appeal.

"I bribed, connived, schemed, and did whatever I had to do to get them off. I don't remember that one went to jail."

On one occasion a millionaire building contractor who was having legal problems with the county asked Gene to represent him.

"I can fix it for you with one phone call," Gene said. "But that call will cost you ten thousand dollars. And I want the money up front."

When the contractor came back with the cash, Gene made the call. The contractor no longer had any legal problems.

"There were even some judges and policemen who came to me for bribes. I didn't have to go to *them*. At Christmas time, for example, they'd hint, heavy-handedly, that it sure would be nice if I'd put a little something in their stockings. And I did.

"I had made it big alright. But it was meaningless and hollow and empty, and I felt terrible inside. And I felt dirty. I wanted love and joy and peace. And I wanted out. But there was no way to get out."

Now Gene's second marriage was failing, and for the same reasons—his selfishness, his ego, his restless quest for meaning in life which still eluded him. Because his emotions were coiled taut as a spring, he was constantly initiating arguments with his wife. Gene and Dorothy decided divorce was preferable to combat.

Gene lost himself in his law practice and continued to party.

"I went back to *la dolce vita*, the sweet life. I remember one party with four hundred guests. There was a big band and lots, I mean lots, of booze. The guests used more than six hundred pounds of ice cubes for the mixed drinks. Some who attended brought marijuana and cocaine. Again, there was the same guest list—judges, lawyers, politicians, bankers and gangsters. Also a liberal sprinkling of prostitutes. That party lasted three days and nights.

"But even with all this jet-set living I missed Dorothy and

the kids. I still loved them. And they, for some reason, still loved me. Dorothy and I started dating again, just like a couple of teenagers. This time we determined to make a go of it, and a couple of months later we were remarried. We started anew. We were really lost, but very much in love."

Gene decided to open his own law office, and the accoutrements were the best money could buy. The furniture was massive and impressive—Gene's desk was eight feet long. He had the most elaborate telephone system available, with automatic dialing equipment that had built-in memory banks and sophisticated eavesdropping devices which enabled him to secretly record conversations. Behind his desk was a walnut paneled refrigerator stocked full of expensive imported champagne, and a gigantic, striking, hand-carved Mexican breakfront filled with every conceivable type of liquor.

He hired the best investigator in Florida, a talented associate, to assist him, and the prettiest secretary in town.

Business started to boom the moment he hung his shingle, and Gene was in a position to set his fees so high that only the rich, no matter how they earned their money, could afford him.

One of his clients was the manager of a five-hundred-dollar-a-night call girl ring. The agreement was that he'd pay Gene one thousand dollars a week for his legal services. Gene's initial assignment was to free one of the manager's girls who'd been arrested.

The obvious first step in the Miami ambience was to try bribing the cop who'd made the arrest.

"No way," the officer said. "She's going to do time. She and her whole gang are a bunch of filthy little tramps. She kneed me and cursed me when I busted her. She's going away."

"The cop was so furious that in this instance he couldn't be bribed," says Gene. "That wasn't like most of the Miami Beach police. They'd take a dive for a nickel."

To fix the case Gene arranged for payment to a judge of one thousand five hundred dollars.

The steady stream of clients brought more luxuries for Gene, including an airplane, a yacht, another house, and a Mercedes-Benz as a companion for his Lincoln.

"I had credit cards and bank accounts. And I belonged to all the groovy little private key clubs and racquet clubs and sportsman's clubs all over southern Florida.

"I had it all."

Gene's office became a way station for criminals *and* police.

"Big-time hoods started hanging around my suite, and drinking my champagne while they put their feet up on my desk.

"All the downtown police hung out there, too. I'd given them keys so that they could come up in the evenings and on weekends with their girl friends or hoodlum pals and booze it up or transact business or play games. Or whatever they wanted."

Gene carried a gun, a .45 Colt Commander. He never used it, but on one occasion he came close.

A Chicago car theft ring sent a "gorilla" to try and convince Gene to return a Cadillac Eldorado that a client of his, a banker, had purchased. The banker, of course, knew the car was stolen, which is why he got it at a bargain price.

"Now they wanted to steal it back, or scare us out of it," Gene says. "A favorite underworld trick. But the goon they sent didn't figure on a lawyer with a .45. When I pointed that big manhole-sized barrel between his eyes there in the swank Miami Beach hotel, he got humble very fast."

Gene also carried a switchblade, and used it more than once. One evening at a bar he got into a fight with a linebacker for the Dallas Cowboys. Three swift punches from the football player's fist sent Gene sprawling to the floor. He got up, put his hand in his pocket and found the knife. His thumb pressed the button, and the blade gleamed angrily. An instant later, Gene slashed out, cutting the athlete's face. Nursing his wound, he left quickly to seek medical attention.

"What an unbelievable life I was living," Gene recalls, "filled with violence, crime, and ungodliness."

His office became a warehouse for the implements of the underworld. Stashed there were machine guns, plastic explosive devices, stolen driver's licenses and passports. Also—drugs.

"Most of my clients were in the drug business, and some of them would pay their fees in cocaine or heroin or hashish.

That's why there was always a lot of it around."

Says Gene: "It was a nightmare world of partying, crime, booze, guns, and drugs—a horrible, brutal world. An incredible life of getting criminals off, getting their cases fixed, living with them, and playing with them.

"The hoods liked me because I was one of them. I got results. They trusted me, and they came to me. And they brought their money in cash or drugs with them when they came.

"There was no one around who could match me in the field of criminal law. In my mind, I'd become Perry Mason. But I was miserable. And, as ever, empty. Many nights I would cry myself to sleep. Life was senseless, psychotic, and worthless.

"So for excitement, I suppose, and possibly for the money —maybe just because I was looking so desperately for something in life—I started getting involved deeper in crime. Deeper and deeper. Bigger and bigger."

For a huge fee, Gene helped devise a scheme for a client who worked for an insurance company and wanted to steal from his own firm. Together, they created phony automobile accidents, phony doctors, and bogus medical and police reports.

"They were all perfect. My client had the authority to sign checks. So he settled each make-believe case by simply bringing his checkbook over and writing a whopping big check to the make-believe lawyers. Then we would forge endorsements on the checks and run them through phony accounts. It was enormously profitable, an absolutely foolproof, perfect crime."

Many of Gene's clients were heavily involved in the smuggling and selling of cocaine, which was a bigger, more lucrative business than heroin. The drug was extremely fashionable among the rich.

Gene would fly with his clients to Bogota, Colombia, the cocaine capitol of the world, and aid them in bootlegging the bitter, lethal narcotic into the U.S.

"It was really easy if you knew how. I was even getting ready to set up my own cocaine processing plant on the outskirts of Bogota. I had a young chemist down there from Miami who was going to run the show on that end."

Gene became so adept at crime that he began devising capers. He explained one idea to a Mafia soldier over champagne in his office.

At the southern tip of Florida, there's a chain of islands called the Keys. On one of those islands was a virtually unprotected bank. The nearest police station was thirty miles to the north.

"Now here's the way to do it," Gene said enthusiastically to his underworld friend, spreading a map of the island before him. "You just blow up the bridge on the north side of the island, then you blow up the bridge on the south side of the island. Voom! Both bridges go at the same time. Then you walk into the bank, deactivate the alarm system, and wipe it out. You leave the island in a speedboat. Two miles out, you sink the boat with a hand grenade just before you take off in an amphibious helicopter which will be waiting for you. They won't know what hit them."

The hood declined the harebrained scheme which, he said, was even too violent for the Mafia.

"I must have been out of my mind," Gene now reflects.

Inevitably, it was only a matter of time until Gene was caught at some type of criminal activity.

His undoing was four and a half pounds of cocaine. Gene had a client who'd been charged with smuggling that amount of the drug. Gene got him off. The grateful client, in lieu of a fee, paid Gene with the cocaine.

The cocaine was worth a fortune, and Gene wanted that fortune. He set about finding a buyer who could handle that much action, getting in touch with one of his underworld buddies.

An eager buyer turned up rapidly. He was a silver-haired, well-manicured man of about sixty who called himself Casey. Gene met him in a cocktail lounge and the deal was quickly consummated.

Not long after, when Gene returned to his office a dozen policemen showed up. Gene knew. He knew Casey was a cop. He knew he'd been double-crossed by his underworld buddy.

Arrested and handcuffed, Gene was taken to jail. Bill Cagney, a federal strike force prosecutor, came to see him.

"You pig!" Cagney declared. "I'm gonna bury you! I'm going to get you the maximum." Cagney was beside himself with rage because Gene had formerly been a public defender and a state prosecutor. He considered Gene a traitor. "I'm gonna bury you," Cagney repeated.

Cagney was as good as his word. Gene was shortly to be buried in the depths of *Springfield.*

Gene had no recourse but to plead guilty. He couldn't buy or talk his way out, not with a dedicated prosecutor who was incorruptible.

He was given fifteen years each on three counts of illegal transfers of cocaine and five years for conspiracy to sell the drug.

The erstwhile "Perry Mason of Florida" now continued telling his story:

"While I prayed, I'd seen my life in all its horrible and tragic reality. Its failure. And I saw myself, for the first time, as I really was—a broken, lonely, abandoned man. Decadent. Tragic.

"How insignificant my Mercedes-Benz seemed to me now —and my airplane—my money—my law degree.

"In my entire life, no one had ever said to me, 'Gene, there's a real God. And He's not just a concept or a word that you banter around. He's real and alive, and He loves you and He cares for you and wants you to be His.' "

Gene, in utter despair, cried out: "Oh, my God, my God! I don't believe You're out there or that You can hear me, but if You are real and if You can hear me, I want You to know that I am so very, very sorry for my whole, miserable, rotten life. If You'll only forgive me and let me start all new, I will give You my whole life—for what little it's worth—as long as I live. I will be totally Yours to do with as You wish, here in prison for fifty years."

Gene's face was a wreath of smiles as he recollected the most dramatic experience of his life.

"You know, Chaplain Ray, there always comes a moment of truth when a man has to face God. But when they slammed the door on me and said fifty years, *that* was my moment of truth.

"I just had to know whether there was a God, and I really meant it from the bottom of my heart as I cried out and pledged my life to Him.

"And I can tell you, my brother, there is a real God. There *is* a real God.

"He came into that tiny cell of mine as I called to Him and touched me in an incredibly powerful way. He anointed me with a love and a joy and a peace and a strength far beyond all human comprehension. He gave me the peace that passeth all understanding.

"When I got up off my knees, the guard who'd been so unfriendly came by. My face was glowing as I told him that God had accepted me. He said, 'Gene, I sure wish I had what you've got.' He was free to go home every night, but I was happier than he was. I was more free than he was and I was doing fifty years."

Gene says he did his time quietly and all of a sudden a year had gone by. Then another year passed. During this time, Gene had been transferred from Springfield Prison to the "Stockade" in Miami, Florida. Soon he was sent to the Federal Prison Camp at Elgin Air Force Base in northern Florida.

"I never even applied for parole—never asked God to get me out. But one day the senior lieutenant came by and said, 'Neill, get your bags together, you're going home.' I'd been granted a parole!"

The Lord has a tremendous sense of humor, Gene says. His last day in prison was Thanksgiving Day.

"Let me tell you, I gave thanks to God as nobody has ever given thanks to God. I sang to Him, and I'll bet I did something, Chaplain Ray, that *you've* never even done. I read the *Scriptures* to God! I sat there in my cell and I'd say, 'Listen to this one, Father.' And I read Him some of my favorite verses. I know it sounds crazy, but He loved it."

Gene had served two years and thirteen days. When he was released, there were thirty Christians, about half of them Baptists, waiting for him at the mesh fence of the stockade.

"I'd never been baptized, so they arranged it. We went down to the ocean and I was immersed, and God was there. It was a wonderful morning, a tremendous morning."

God then called Gene and his family to southern California. For a week or so, he couldn't get a job.

"I finally found the greatest job in the world—at least my kids thought it was—driving an ice cream truck with a bell—one of those that goes around the neighborhood selling Popsicles. I sold ice cream all summer, and told all the kids on my route about Jesus. That was something—the former 'Perry Mason of Florida' witnessing to everyone he met while selling ice cream."

Gene thought that low-paying job superior to his career as an influential, wealthy lawyer. His money had vanished, blown away by the winds of overspending and credit buying. Money was no longer important to Gene, because the focus of his life had changed. Now he was living for God instead of fronting for criminals.

God had a new calling for Gene as he continued to get his bearings in the free world after his imprisonment. "I went into the ministry full time. It's a faith ministry. I travel around preaching and teaching in churches all over the country and in as many foreign countries as possible."

While he was in prison, Gene enrolled in the extension program of the Liberty Bible College in Pensacola, Florida, completing the eighteen-month program.

His wife went to the school, tape-recorded the lectures, and sent them to Gene, who listened to them avidly in his cell. He took all the exams and earned an *A* average.

"In fact, I remember the teacher was almost fussing at the class because the students' grades hadn't been too high. I heard him say on a tape, 'You all ought to be ashamed of yourselves. Most of you are doing *C* work, and there's Gene Neill in prison who's got the only *A.* '

"I guess I had more time to study than they did. I literally read the entire Bible more than fifty times in prison. Each complete reading took two weeks." Gene completed his training for the ministry at the Melodyland School of Theology in

Anaheim, California. "I teased the fellow who ordained me. I said, 'You know, I've probably read the Bible more times than you have.' He just laughed and answered, 'You probably have.'

"Chaplain Ray, the Bible materials you sent me after I wrote you from prison truly blessed me.

"The average prison inmate reads seven times as much as the average man in the street, and ten times as much as he himself will read after he's released from prison.

"Prisoners are crying for printed material. They are desperate for Bibles. Other inmates used to beg me to try and get them a Bible or to share mine.

"I hope your ministry reaches the point where you can supply Bibles, Bible dictionaries, your magazine, and your map of the Holy Land, to every inmate in the country."

Gene has preached from California to Puerto Rico to the Soviet Union.

"I was in Russia for three months in 1976, and communist agents followed me and harassed me. Several times they crashed into my meetings with machine guns and attack dogs!

"But the secret police didn't intimidate me, nor those large crowds who came to hear me preach the gospel. There are more Christians, millions of them, in Russia than people realize, although the official government policy for more than sixty years has been atheism.

"Through an interpreter, I preached Jesus, uplifted His name, and ignored the attempts to frighten me off.

"At the first opportunity I plan to go back. They need Jesus as much in Moscow and Stalingrad as they do in Los Angeles and New York."

Gene Neill showed his Christian courage in Moscow as well as in that Springfield, Missouri, prison cell when he came to God. There's no finer soldier of the Lord anywhere than Gene.

"Jesus came for people like me," Gene concludes, "people in prison cells, sick people, people in need, and people who are in sorrow. That's why Jesus died. He died for people like me who needed Him.

"Jesus isn't only on the mountain tops. He's down there with you when you're on your knees and you really need Him—

when you're crying out for Him.

"He's always there . . . waiting."

The sum of Gene's life is best expressed in one of his favorite Bible verses, John 8:36: "If the Son therefore shall make you free, ye shall be free indeed."

9

"Dear Chaplain Ray"

The letters flood in from inmates in penal institutions from Maine to California, Florida to Washington. Each letter is given a personal reply, for it is all the work of God and one of the most important parts of my ministry.

What do prisoners write about? The letters, self-explanatory, speak for themselves.

Let me share some of them with you:

Praise God! Sir, I wrote sometime ago and received a Bible and dictionary. Thank you! Now once again I'm asking for a Bible, a dictionary, a calendar and map. You see, I had them sitting on my bed and went out of my cell for a walk. When I returned, they, among other things, were missing. Now I feel totally lost without my Bible. So please would you send me another as soon as possible.

When I first wrote nine months ago, I was lost. But with people like you I have found hope, peace and freedom. Thank you very much. May God bless and protect you and yours.

I am in the Lexington County Jail, and my family left me here with nothing. They moved away a few months ago to another state. My father said that he didn't want anything to do with me. So I have one thing on my mind: that is to study the Bible and learn, and make something of myself. So if you would, I would like you to send me a Bible and Bible study books, so I can learn about God.

I am sitting in my cell this night and look at a Book another inmate gave me. It seems as though each time I look, or pick it up, or touch a Bible, I get this cold feeling up and down my back, and I start to cry. It's true—God and I have never really been together in my life, because I have lived a life of crime almost all of the way.

But when I go to sleep, I dream of God, and I see myself preaching to large groups of people—I don't know where. I have never given a sermon in my life. I feel this force; but when I get down on my knees, all I know how to do is cry, and lose out on what I want to say.

Chaplain Ray, I'm thirty-three years old and have been in prison for close to twenty years off and on. I'm only two years and nine months away from being out of here completely. But I'm ashamed of my past, and I'm sorry for my wrongs. I've asked for forgiveness; yet I feel this great weight upon my shoulders and I don't know what to do. I have done so much wrong in my life that I feel no forgiveness from God will ever come, as much as I ask. Maybe I'm asking the wrong way.

Sir, do you think I could preach to people in this state of mind? I've had only a little bit of schooling, but I feel that if ever I was put before a large group of people, I would know what to say, and how to say it and express the true feelings of God. Does this mean that I'm crazy?

Can I be helped to go forward in life for God? To be a man who can spread the word of God? Can I live out the rest of my life in true love for every living thing? These are some of the things that keep going through my mind. I can't answer these questions at all. What should I do? Can you help me in any way?

Sir, I'm sorry, but I did not mean to take up so much of your time. It's just that I've felt this for so long that I felt that I must ask someone.

Can an ex-inmate become a minister of God—to carry His cross, and take some of the weight off others?

I wish I could hear from you.

Four days ago today I gave myself to Christ the Lord! And let me tell you, I am happy I did. But, Chaplain Ray, I have a problem. It is hard for me to understand all the words in the Bible. I have heard from others that there is a Bible dictionary. If it won't be too much of a problem or cost, would you please send me a copy?

I will tell you a little about myself. I am twenty years old. I was born in Texas, and lived there until I was seventeen years old. I joined the Navy to get away from my family. I was working for my father six days a week, from three in the morning until six at night, in a bakery my father owns. I was forced to quit school after nine years of it because of my work. Well, I went into the Navy, and I was arrested on five counts of arson and sent to prison for ten years.

Four days ago I got down on my knees in my cell and asked Christ to come into my life. I always thought that because I was a sinner, God would have nothing to do with me. But now I know differently. Praise the Lord, I know different. Well, Chaplain Ray, I have to leave now.

P.S. And Chaplain Ray, I sure would like to have a cross for my cell. Thank you.

At the present time I am in Pontiac State Prison in Illinois. I am trying to pick up the broken pieces of my life and put them back together. I know the only real way to do this is by putting all my faith in Jesus and trying to do His will. My life has been one big mess. I would really appreciate any kind of literature that you have and your sending it to me. Thank you for reading this.

I'm a prisoner in the woman's jail in Cincinnati, Ohio.

I have been in and out of trouble since I was twenty years old. I'm twenty-eight years old now and tired. Since I've been in jail this time, I've turned to Jesus. At first I was afraid to because I felt I had no right, but I was told that I was not the judge of that, so, reluctantly, I started reading about God and Jesus. Now I want to learn more— all I can. It is very possible that I may get probation, but I know I'm still weak, so I don't want to go out there immediately. Plus, like I said, I want to learn more about Jesus Christ. You see, since I've turned to Jesus, I've never felt better, and I want to tell others about Him. That's why I want to learn more.

Would you send me a Bible, a Bible dictionary, and other literature? I wish you would, because I want to learn and understand everything I can about Jesus. Thank you so very much.

I'm a born-again Christian, but I'd drifted away from my Lord Jesus and therefore got myself into trouble. However, I got right with God before I was ever sentenced. I don't have a long time to serve in prison, but I know I had to be broken down in order to come to my senses. It's hard to believe I'm taking it so well. I've just turned it all over to the Lord, and I've got such a hunger to absorb His teachings. Sometimes I just can't read your literature fast enough to see what is said next.

May God bless you in your work for Him.

I am a prisoner at the federal penitentiary at Terre Haute, Indiana, and I receive a copy of your magazine, *Prison Evangelism,* every month. It sure helps me to read about others who have the same kind of problems that I have had. I am serving twenty-one years for kidnapping and I am far from proud of it, but it would never have taken place if I had not been on dope and whisky at the time. But now I have a new life here since I have Jesus to help me carry the load. I feel free even though I am locked up.

I am taking a Bible correspondence course, and I would like to ask you if I could have a Bible dictionary. It sure would help me out a lot, and it would be greatly appreciated if you could send me a copy.

Well, I will close this and I will be praying for you to be able to keep up the good work, and I wish that you pray for me, and help me through my hour of need. May God bless you.

Every day I read my Bible and pray to God to keep His healing hand on me and guide me through each day while I'm here. Please pray for me, Chaplain Ray, because next month I go for a sentence reduction to get my sentence cut in half. I received a 2 to 4 year term for forgery.

I attend church here every week and Bible classes on Tuesdays and Fridays to get to know Jesus Christ better.

I pray that God be with you and your wife. Please pray for me and my fellow inmates. I'll be waiting to hear from you.

I want to thank you with all my heart for the Bible that I just received from you.

God is needed in this place so much because there are so few Christians in here. I was reading my Bible today and a guy passed my cell. A few minutes later he came back with a couple of his friends and just stood there and started laughing at me. I told them that it was the devil that was putting them up to that, and then they left; and one of them came back and said he was sorry.

There is so much that God has done for me; and I do thank God for saving my soul and for putting my feet on His solid Rock. He has made me a new person and has started me on a new life.

You don't know me, but I heard a lot about you. I don't have too much to say, because once you're in prison, you seem to run out of words.

What words I am writing I have learned myself how to spell by reading a lot. I come from a small town. My mother raised me until I was sixteen. Then she passed away. Then I was on my own. I did pretty good until I got in with the wrong crowd. And here I am, doing two and a half years State time, about seven blocks from what I once called my hometown. When my mother passed away, I seemed to drift away from my brothers and sisters. They didn't want me around anymore. Anyway, I'm hanging onto the only thing I have—it is the Lord, and I will keep hanging on, too, because I know with Him I'll make it.

The purpose of this letter is to request a copy of the latest edition of your magazine, but I have no money. My address is at the top of this page. I have to go now. Smile, God loves you.

I have been in different places, such as Cumberland County Prison at Carlisle, Pennsylvania, and also Camp Hill for a month and a half. I was then transferred to Fairview State Hospital for the Criminally Insane. Now I am at Huntingdon State Correctional Institution. I was locked up almost two years ago. I am now serving a double life sentence in this prison.

Chaplain Ray, please pray for me. I do need someone to keep me going. Jesus will help me, I know He will. But there're times I really feel depressed and angry with myself, and I take it out on others; and I do know it is wrong. I have asked Jesus to come into my life, but somewhere I feel I'm missing something. Can you help me to find that something? I'm going to pray about it as soon as I am finished with this letter. Please! I need someone to guide me and see me through.

I don't know if you remember me or not, but you did give me a great deal of assistance when I first came to this dreadful place they call a jail. I've often written you and you've always written back and been a real pal.

I've been meaning to get back to you but couldn't. Oh, well, on to the reason for this letter. I wanted mostly to tell you that last month, Jesus Christ came into my heart. I finally opened up and accepted Him as my *Source* and *Savior*. Praise the Lord, He means so much to me. You were a great help getting me started in the right direction.

There is a guy here who would also like to get started in God's direction. Would you send him a Bible and other religious material? I know he can be richly blessed.

I am an inmate in the Missouri Training Center for Men here at Moberly, Missouri. You see, Chaplain Ray, I may be released on parole next month, and even if I don't make it, I only have two and a half years left on a fifteen-year sentence. But my parole officer told me if I don't make it next month, he is pretty sure I will within the next year. I know I should be happy and not have any worries because I just about have my bit completed. But for some strange reason, I'm not happy. I find myself not being able to sleep at night. I smoke almost two packs of cigarettes a day and get so nervous at times my hands start shaking. Before this, I have never been a person to worry or be scared of anything.

I have been in and out of jails and institutions since I was thirteen years old, and I am twenty-six years old now. I caught my first big hit when I was seventeen years old—it was six years for burglary and escape. I was sent to the Algoa Reformatory and was later transferred to the main prison in Jefferson City, Missouri, after I got into a lot of trouble and beat up another inmate with a steel mop handle. I completed the six years without a parole and was released on September 1, 1970. I was arrested on September 10, 1970 for eight robberies and one first-degree murder. I only got time for one robbery, and that's the fifteen-year bit I am finishing up now.

I have never really had a job on the streets before, but I also know I have as good a chance of making it outside as anyone that comes out of here, because I have not wasted my time. Since I have been confined, I have completed high school and have taken some college courses. I am really sure I won't ever be back to prison, because I don't have any desire whatsoever to steal again or ever use drugs. It's been several months since I've had any drugs, and they are very plentiful around this institution.

But I still have this cold lost feeling like there is still something wrong. I would also like to say that I was raised in a very religious family until I left home, so I know there is a God somewhere, even though I have tried to tell myself there isn't. I think I just may need to find God and everything may be okay for me, but I have a problem. For some reason I just can't make myself go to the chapel or do anything to find Him. Yet I know that's what I want. I keep thinking that my friends are going to say I hung tough until right at the last, then go weak.

Chaplain Ray, I need some kind of help. I would like to know just how you would handle the situation I am in if it were you. Also if you happen to have an extra Bible laying around, I would really like to have one.

I would like to thank you very much for reading this letter and anything you can do to help me, even though I am not a Christian yet.

I am writing you to ask a prayer for me and my family. I am in the Penitentiary for Women in Virginia. I would like to have a Bible, a Bible Dictionary and a Holy Land map. A friend here told me about you and said that you were a wonderful person.

I came to know God on November 16, 1975, and I have been happy ever since. I want to know more and more about Him, because He is wonderful; He is a good God. So will you please pray for me, and I will do likewise.

I'm now serving time in this North Carolina prison. My sentence is fourteen years, and I have found God since coming to prison. My wife and family are standing by me, and I thank God for that. I really didn't know God before, but now I have Him in my heart, and it feels good. I don't know how I lived all those years without God, and when I think about it, I break down and cry. It is going to be awhile before I get out, but with God I can make it. When I get out, I want to do God's work, but the best place to start is here. I have turned my life over to God, and will live it for Him.

Chaplain Ray, if you could, please write to me. I would be most thankful to you, and please pray for me. I have to close for now, and hope to hear from you soon.

I am finally back in North Carolina, doing a sentence I escaped from on September 26, 1968. I finished my federal time on September 26, 1975, and was returned to North Carolina State Penitentiary on September 30, 1975.

If possible, I would like you to do something for me.

I have a brother, who is doing time for robbery at Southampton Farm in Capron, Virginia. It's his first time in prison, and he is only nineteen years of age. I would like to send him a package and a nice AM-FM radio, but I am unable to and our parents aren't either.

Before my brother is deeper in sin, I would like you to try and get to know him and help him out as much as you can, before he winds up learning a lot more the hard way as I did. I myself have been locked up and away from home ever since I was seventeen. I am now twenty-seven. I have been through the ropes. I love my brother a lot and sure hate to see or hear of him going from bad to worse.

Will you write him, send him a Bible and things about Christ to read, also send him a package for me? I'm sure he will be very grateful and appreciate it ever so much.

I myself would like to receive a package from your prison ministry, and, if possible, also a nice gold chain and cross.

My Mom and Dad really can't help me and my younger brother. At times I really feel as if no one really loves or cares for us. I believe I might be too far gone, but there is still a lot of hope for my brother. Any help that you may be able to give my brother and me will be greatly appreciated—more than you may realize.

I sincerely do hope to hear from you soon, and I hope that you will try to help my brother.

I'm incarcerated in the Jackson County Jail, Kansas City, Missouri.

It's so wonderful to know that we have such a wonderful friend as Jesus. This may sound odd, but I have thanked Jesus for my capture, for it has opened my eyes. I am an alcoholic and was severely under the influence when my crime occurred, which I know is no excuse. By the time you receive this, I will be in the Missouri State Prison, paying my debt to society by serving a three-year term. I thank Jesus for letting the judge be so lenient with me.

Soon after I enter the prison, I will write you another letter. If you are ever at this institution, I would love to meet you in person. And I would like to receive any publications you print in the future.

I have spent seventeen of my earlier years behind bars. I was released from the Missouri Prison thirty-two years ago. Also, I have spent seven years in the Oklahoma Prison, being out of there for eighteen years. Now I have to go back for three years. But I have no fear as I know Jesus will always be near. I have asked Him for help so many times, that I wonder if I still have the right to. But He never turns me down. He works in such marvelous ways. I've said it so many times and shall continue to do so: Satan can't build a fire hot enough to make me defy my God in heaven.

I will close for this time. May God be with you always, and may He bless you in health and happiness and in everything you may undertake. You shall always be in my prayers.

I have a good story to tell everyone. I got out of the army in 1942, and got a one-year sentence in La Grange, Kentucky. I served nine months and twenty-four days. Then I got three years in 1944 for car theft and was sent to Brushy Mountain Prison in Tennessee. I did twenty-four months in the coal mines digging coal. My task was 8,000 pounds a day; it comes to four tons. If you missed reaching that, they whipped you with a six-foot strap at night. I got out in 1946. Then I got twelve to sixty-six years in 1947 for three shootings with intent to commit first-degree murder. I served seven years and one month. I made parole in 1954. I was on parole for six years. Then I got ninety-nine years for first-degree murder on circumstantial evidence and my past record. I was sent to Nashville State Prison in 1960, and I have been locked up ever since.

I wish you would come and write a story about me, for I have completed twenty-eight years of my sentence. You see, altogether I've got 165 more years to serve. But the most wonderful thing happened to me last month. I confessed my sins to Jesus and I was saved. I am living for the Lord now. After all these years I finally found Jesus. I was twenty-five years old when I got all this time in 1947. Now I am fifty-three years old.

Chaplain Ray, I do hope and pray that you will write my story so all the young people can see just how easy it is to mess up your life.

I wish you would send me a gift package since all in my family are dead. I don't have anyone.

Chaplain, I really don't know why I'm writing you. I never have known too much about being a Christian, but I do believe there is a God or something out there. Chaplain, I am twenty years old and I have a twenty-five year sentence and only have about a year and a half of it done. Since I was put in this cell I haven't seen or talked to anyone yet. My parents hardly ever write, and I need something to do with my time, so you may get a few letters from me. I hardly know anyone else to write to, and if I did write, I probably wouldn't hear anything back.

Chaplain, please send me all the reading material you can. I don't have a Bible and if you have an extra one, please send it. I hope I'm not asking too much of you, sir. I feel that I am, but I don't really know. I hope not.

A girl in the next cell said she had a Bible and she let me read it! She told me about you, and she said you sent it to her.

I've been in and out of jail for a long time. I just got out about two months ago, and I started going to church with my grandmother. I really liked it in a way. At first I felt like a fool. None of my friends go to church and I thought they would think of me as a fool, so I didn't tell them. Maybe I should have. Then I might not be here. But everything was going wrong!

So now I'm back in jail. I still would like to learn about God and some of the things He has done. I really don't care what my friends think of me anymore. They can't be friends if they get me locked up. And the only true friend I have is God! So I want to find out everything I can about Him. So if you could send me a Bible, I would be truly thankful.

Sir, I guess I have never really thought about my life and what is going to happen to it after death.

You know, it is kind of funny—every time I see something with your name on it, I read it and really get a warm feeling down deep inside. I am doing a two-year sentence in the State Oklahoma Prison. I am twenty-five as I had my birthday in here. This is the second time I am in a prison. It seems like I would have learned. But, sir, I have been missing something down deep inside all my life. More or less I was trying to find peace within myself and happiness and, most of all, love. It always did seem that when I would go on the right track, I would end in the wrong way again.

The prison here has given me a lot of time to think. I think I'm lucky, since I will be able to have another chance on the streets. Hopefully, I will be discharged in four or five months or make parole before then. I keep thinking about what I will do when I do get out of here, and I keep coming up with, "I don't know." When I do leave here, I will have nothing—a little money but no family. I've got the feeling that God will look out for me and help me out, because I know now what I am missing. I guess God has been waiting for me to realize this.

There are about 1,500 convicts here, and each one of us looks for the day we can receive our freedom once again. But a lot of us have another freedom God has given us—one that no man can take away. The bars and the guards look bad to us each day, but we meet each day that comes. Even though we are in prison here, God is so strong. I can feel Him every day of my life.

Please respond to this letter, Chaplain Ray.

You are doing a wonderful thing. I love you for this as a prisoner, because I know God is with you. I hope someday I can meet you in person!

I am twenty-four and have been running from the law for three years. I know I am a sinner and I want to be saved. My husband and I went all over the country writing bad checks. So now I am in jail. I have six months here in the Workhouse. Then I have to go to court on federal charges and I have some other state charges. I got so tired of running, I am glad it is over. I wrote my father-in-law about you. He is a preacher in Grapevine, Texas. I love this man because he has tried to help us before, but I wouldn't listen. But I am ready to accept Jesus as my Savior.

Chaplain Ray, will you please send me a Bible? I would appreciate it.

For the past twenty years I've been confined to various prisons for a number of different crimes.

Soon I will be released. Since my imprisonment, my only hope and desire was what type of criminal activity I would involve myself in.

In my thirty-six years on earth I have never felt full, complete, and worthy. The other day a fellow inmate gave me your magazine, *Prison Evangelism.* After reading your magazine, it finally dawned on me why I was lacking in fullness, completeness and worthiness: Complete indifference to God. Henceforth, I will dedicate myself to the Good Lord until my life expires. I have no money, so therefore I would be grateful if you would send me at no cost *Prison Evangelism,* a Bible dictionary, and other reading material you can spare. I shall donate to your worthy cause when I am released.

I am a prisoner at the Washington State Reformatory. I find it so encouraging to listen to your broadcast every day at 10 A.M. on KBLE. As I listen to all the testimonies from inmates inside prison walls, I'm persuaded that creed, color, social status, or incarceration can't prevent the changing power of Jesus Christ. He looks into the heart. He's the same yesterday, today, and forever. I don't personally know one of the inmates who testified through your broadcasts, yet I know we share unity through Jesus Christ our Lord. I thank God for saving me from myself and the bondage of Satan. Through drugs I almost ruined my life, but, He set me free and caused my feet to walk in straight paths. Now, I'm going to be married, and no longer need drugs to experience joy, for the joy of the Lord is my strength.

I accepted the Lord right here behind prison walls. My fiancee did too. You should see the looks we get as she walks into the visiting room with her Bible. And when we bow our heads to pray, some don't know what to do at times. We love the Lord, and are grateful for the work He's doing in us.

If you could send me a Bible dictionary and a concordance I would certainly appreciate that a lot. I find that as I find different verses His word talks just to me. I thank God today that because He lives, I can face tomorrow. I'm thanking God today for your ministry and will be with you in prayer, Chaplain Ray. God bless you real good.

I had to write to you tonight Chaplain Ray, for I was sitting in my cell and feeling lonesome and thinking about home. So I started crying. Please, Chaplain Ray, pray for me and send me a prayer for I do want to know God. My life is so lonely and miserable. God bless you and your wonderful work.

I'm seventeen years old. My number here is 19581. I met a young man in here who's told me so much about what the Lord can do for me. At first I really didn't care, but now I do want to meet the Lord. I told my friend that if he'd write this letter to you for me I promised I'd start going to church, and I'd start reading the Bible as soon as my friend teaches me to read. I thank him very much for taking his time to teach me how to read. He said the door is open. Now all I have to do is walk through it. And he said this, and I'll never forget it: "If I really want to read, I have to put faith into it." And he said, "If you want to learn I'll help you, but you also have to help yourself." He wants to get his high school equivalency, so when he gets out he can go to theology school for 2 years in Texas.

Brother Ray, could you please send me a Bible and some material? When I learn to read, this material will come in handy.

Well, I've been in and out of jail most of my life. I never could follow that road of righteousness until I met this one man that gave me faith in Christ. He said the Lord died on the cross and shed His blood for me. The least I could do is serve Him now. I hope you pray for this young man so that he can help other people besides me. And I also hope that you will pray for me so that I may learn the laws of God and learn how to read too. I hope that you put this letter in *Prison Evangelism,* so I can tell our brother inmates here that there is someone who cares for them, wants to help them, and loves them very much. This wonderous man is Jesus Christ our Lord.

I am an inmate at the Federal Youth Center in Ashland, Kentucky. I was sentenced for four years. This is the first time that I have ever been sent to a prison. However, I have been in and out of jails since I was eighteen. I think my record reflects over forty arrests in the past six years. That is not counting when I was a kid.

Ever since my mother died in 1959, my life hasn't really meant too much to me. I was always being bounced around from one relative to another because my father was in and out of prison so much. I grew up on sex, booze, and dope. And I had to rob and steal to supply my needs. But I never knew what happiness was. Even when I was high on drugs, I wasn't really happy. I would see people attending church and think that they were nuts.

When I was fifteen I quit school and started traveling with county fairs which added a little pleasure to my life. After I was beaten for stealing a speaker from a tent, I went to Indianapolis, Indiana, to stay with my grandmother.

It wasn't anytime before my police record began to grow again. So I returned to my old neighborhood in Columbus, Ohio. In 1972, I ran away with a girl who I used to go to school with. We returned to Indianapolis, and when she was of age we got married. We once again returned to Columbus, Ohio. Our marriage lasted only four months because of my drinking and dope.

I was arrested on two felony charges. While I was in jail my wife wrote me a letter saying that she wanted a divorce. It was then that I took a serious look at God. I started to read the Bible and attend Bible study in the Chaplain's office. I don't even think that I had ever heard of Jesus then. But He soon became my only hope.

When I went to court five months later, through God's love and mercy, I received probation. God continued to answer my prayers and my wife and I soon got back together.

Everything was fine until I started drinking again. We were together for four months and then we separated. I tried to get high on drugs to hide from God because I couldn't stand to live with myself.

It has been over two years now since our separation. But I praise the Lord! God has forgiven me and given me a new life. Even though in prison, I'm free! And although I seem to have many problems, God has given me joy through Jesus.

I am writing to you from Bexar County Jail in San Antonio. I am nineteen years old and have only been in jail once before for just a few days.

I have not paid much attention to the Bible in the past, although I like to read Psalms. I used to go to church when I was younger but not lately.

I was talking to an older man here who has been in a lot of prisons most of his life. He said he became a born-again Christian through something that happened a few months ago. I don't know just what he means by born again, but he said you could furnish me with a Bible and some books to read, and I would soon learn if I wanted to for sure. I will appreciate having a Bible of my own in here.

How are you, dear brother! I'm in the Oregon State Penitentiary doing fifteen years, but I'm not unhappy anymore. I've found Jesus in here and now I want to use my time to learn more about my Jesus. I was wondering if you could be so kind as to send me a Bible and any other material you might be able to send. I just wanted to find out more about this wonderful Man who just saved a man like me! I've told everyone about it, but some think I'm nuts. Others think it's great. We all praise Jesus for He's a great guy and I'm going to serve Him from now on instead of Satan. Praise God! So anything you could send me would be great. I'm praying for you and your fine ministry. God bless you, Chaplain Ray.

I am an inmate at the Southern Ohio Correctional Facility in Lucasville, Ohio. I have heard your prison broadcast and I was very pleased. Chaplain Ray, I am doing hard time. My cell is in Protective Custody and I can't even attend church. So I hold church with just me and the Lord in this 6 × 10 cell. Death Row is right next door. I've heard you refer to Death Row many times and I've heard you speak of the miracles God can work, even in prison, and even on Death Row. Actually I feel dead inside already. But with your help and from what I've heard you say, well, I'm ready Chaplain Ray, I'm ready to live again. In Christ's name. Please help me.

I have completed a beginner's Bible course, and I am taking another more advanced one as soon as I can get it. I love what I'm learning about the Bible. But I only have a New Testament and part of it is missing. I would very much like to receive a Bible and a Bible dictionary from you. Because of a lifetime of neglect I have a lot to learn about Christianity if the good Lord's willing to let me learn.

So please pray for me, Chaplain Ray, and help me accept Christ into my life and learn to be a good Christian. I do hope you can help me. I sold my dinner for a stamp to write this letter. But I trust in the Lord, and I feel it was well worth the sacrifice. Jesus fasted, didn't He? Yes, so I feel no remorse.

In fact, I feel glad. I won't ask you to send me a stamp so I can write again. I have asked enough already. I'll just trust the Lord to provide.

I am, however, very anxious for your reply, and I hope to receive a Bible and Bible dictionary. To me a gift like this is made to order and will make me happier than a pair of shoes to a boy who never had none.

Also, help me find Jesus. I feel a need for Him in my life—a deep and urgent need.

Thank you so much, Chaplain Ray, and may God bless you.

10

The "Catch Me" Killer

"Please catch me . . . please . . . I just killed three people, and I may kill tonight, too," said the strained voice on the telephone.

"You must be kidding," Deputy Sheriff James Rice replied.

"I'm serious. Catch me, please . . . come and get me before I kill again."

The caller then hung up abruptly, without identifying himself or his whereabouts. The date was August 12, 1968. The time: 6:18 P.M. The place: Hollywood, Florida.

Deputy Rice mentioned the call to Harold Lemore, a fellow officer working the complaint desk with him. They weren't sure what to make of it. There had been no other reports in the county of a triple killing. The caller could be a practical joker with a warped sense of humor, or, more frighteningly, he may have been telling the truth.

The same voice was back on the phone shortly, at 6:30 P.M. This time Deputy Lemore took the call.

"Rice?" the voice said.

"He's on another line."

"If you want to find those bodies . . . go to the airport . . . one in the water . . . one by the road, by the highway . . . hurry . . . catch me, please . . . please catch me . . ."

Again the caller hung up without disclosing his name or location.

Robert John Erler, after placing the two frantic phone calls to the sheriff from a public booth, drove to his trailer home on the beach. He felt a little better now; some of his anger was dissipated by making the phone calls. He would not kill again tonight. He was too tired to do anything but sleep. Besides, he had a demanding job to go to in the morning.

Robert John Erler, the confessed slayer of three, was a member of the Hollywood, Florida, police department. He was, in fact, so adept at apprehending lawbreakers that on the force and in the local press he was known as *Super Cop!*

Thus began one of the most bizarre murder cases in the annals of American crime—a case that would not come full circle until Bob Erler gave me his personal confession seven years after he became a murderer.

The morning after he phoned the sheriff, Bob, dressed in his police uniform, rushed to a wooded area near the highway, hoping one of his victims was still alive. He examined the body of blonde, twelve-year-old Merilyn Clark. Bob remembered firing four bullets from a 22-caliber pistol into the left side of her head. A fifth shot had torn through her cheek. The girl was dead.

Identifying himself this time, Bob phoned the desk at the Hollywood Police Department to report he had discovered the body of a young girl.

The girl's mother, Mrs. Dorothy Clark, had been found at the airport. Bob had also fired five bullets into her head. Miraculously, she had survived. No third body was ever located.

Bob Erler was among the officers assigned to find Merilyn Clark's killer and the would-be murderer of her mother. But this was one case *Super Cop* Bob Erler didn't solve.

After participating in the investigation for three weeks, Bob decided to quit his job, because his mother was in a Phoenix, Arizona, hospital, suffering from cancer.

In Phoenix, Bob visited his mother daily. One night, after returning from the hospital, he switched on the television set to watch the news.

"We interrupt this program for a special bulletin," the announcer said. "Police and the FBI have begun a search throughout Phoenix for a former Green Beret, a killer who vows never to be taken alive. His name is Robert John Erler. . . ."

Bob Erler blinked. It didn't register at first. He called the TV station to check the name. Yes, the authorities were combing Phoenix for Robert John Erler. Next, Bob Erler phoned the sheriff. A half hour later, he was in custody. He waived extradition, was returned to Florida, and was charged with second-degree murder.

How was Bob Erler linked to the crime? As he would soon discover, the damning evidence came from five Hollywood Police Department officers. The sheriff's communications system routinely recorded all incoming calls. When the tape had been played for Bob's fellow officers in an effort to identify the voice, to their horror they discovered it was Bob's. They all agreed, unmistakably and reluctantly, that the voice indeed was that of Bob Erler.

Unable to post a $35,000 bond, Bob spent seven months in jail, awaiting his trial.

His cellmate told him, "Boy, when you get to prison they're going to kill you for being a cop. You're marked for death."

But Bob Erler didn't think he was going to prison. In his own mind, he was innocent; by now he had washed from his consciousness any memory of murder.

The trial lasted a week. The star witness for the prosecution was Mrs. Dorothy Clark. She was still recovering from her wounds, but was able to testify.

She immediately identified Bob Erler as her assailant and the murderer of her daughter.

They'd met on the beach. Mrs. Clark remembered Bob was wearing a khaki police shirt. He told Mrs. Clark and her daughter that sleeping on the beach wasn't permitted. The mother and daughter were in Florida from Georgia, looking for work and almost penniless. Bob Erler had offered to let them sleep in his trailer nearby. He said his wife and twenty-two-month-old son would be there. Mrs. Clark and Merilyn accepted his offer of hospitality, but when they reached the trailer, they found no one present.

Bob Erler promptly exposed himself, and told Merilyn, "Your mother's going to take care of me."

They left the trailer, with Bob following them. The last thing she remembered, Mrs. Clark testified, was her daughter saying, "Mama, you sure know how to pick the kooks."

Mrs. Clark was certain Bob Erler was the man who killed her daughter. "I'll never forget the mean expression in his eyes," she said.

After Mrs. Clark's testimony, the five Hollywood Police Department officers paraded to the stand. Each identified the voice of Bob Erler as it was played on a tape-recorder.

When Bob got on the stand, he denied everything, insisting he had never seen Mrs. Clark until her appearance in court.

In his closing argument, Bob's lawyer said, "This little boy, this boy who has been besieged by troubles is innocent." At that point, Mrs. Clark bolted from the courtroom in disgust.

A jury of six men, all fathers, deliberated for two hours and came back with a verdict of guilty.

Judge E. Summers Sheffey sentenced Bob to ninety-nine years and six months at hard labor. The sentence meant that Bob would have to spend at least thirty-three years in prison before he could be paroled. If it had been a life sentence, he would have been eligible for parole in seven years.

Bob Erler—still declaring himself innocent—was removed from the courtroom in shackles. Though at that moment he was a beaten man, his story had just begun.

Bob was given special permission from the warden to telephone me on Thanksgiving Day in August 1975.

"Chaplain, are you coming to Florida soon, or could you make a special trip to see me? I need to talk with you. If I'm going to be a Christian, I must tell the truth."

Less than forty-eight hours later, I was in the chapel with Bob at the Florida State Prison. (I'd had a few minutes to say hello and pray with an old friend, Murf the Surf.) Bob Erler told me he was ready to confess. I had interviewed Bob once before, and in that interview he had continued to maintain his innocence, saying his mind was blurred and fogged insofar as Mrs. Clark and her daughter were concerned.

But now Bob was telling me that he was the "Catch Me" killer. It was his first admission to anyone of his guilt.

"I am a guilty man," he said. "I confess my sins, not only to Jesus Christ, but to the world. I have transgressed. I have nobody to blame but Bob Erler. I let the devil get hold of me and I just"—tears welled in his eyes—"what can I say?"

After Bob composed himself, he had a great deal to say. He had walked a bewildering path in his journey from *Super Cop,* to convicted murderer, to the throne of God.

Bob came from a large, closely knit family. He had four younger brothers and two older sisters. The family had migrated from Massachusetts to Arizona.

"My father was hardheaded. He didn't believe in any kind of religion whatsoever. He was, if anything, extremely antireligious."

Bob grew up to become a rugged, extremely good-looking young man. At the age of thirty-four, he had a ruddy complexion, sandy hair, was a solid five feet nine, and weighed 225 pounds. As someone said of him, "He's built like a Sherman tank."

Bob conditioned himself physically, becoming an expert in both karate and judo. He served with conspicuous gallantry in Vietnam as a Green Beret. After his discharge, he decided to become a policeman. He applied and was readily accepted on the Hollywood force.

His reputation as a *Super Cop* grew quickly. He had a sixth sense for the detection of criminals.

Once, while riding late at night with another officer along a highway on patrol, Bob said, "I think we should stop that car ahead of us."

"Why?" his partner asked skeptically.

"Because it's a stolen car."

Bob had no proof—it wasn't on the *hot sheet* that listed stolen cars.

Bob's partner laughed and said, "Why don't we get a cup

of coffee? We'll stop one later."

"No, stop that vehicle."

They did. Their haul: five prisoners who'd escaped from a nearby jail!

"Shortly after that," says Bob, "I was on my own, driving down a street and I had the feeling, again for some unknown reason, that I should stop the vehicle ahead of me. I did stop it, and it turned out to be a stolen car that had been involved in a hit-and-run accident and an armed robbery. I captured the three suspects in the car."

On another occasion, Bob was on patrol on U.S. 1 at four o'clock in the morning.

"That feeling came over me once more. This time, it said I should recheck the window and screen door in the back of a roadhouse. When I arrived, I threw my patrol car spotlight on the window, which I had checked fifteen or twenty minutes before. The screen was ripped off and the window broken.

"Just then, one suspect came around the corner and fired a shot at me that went right over the top of my head. There were three of them, and we had a shoot-out. I took them all as prisoners. I just knew definitely they were there."

There were many similar incidents, and they earned Bob his reputation as a *Super Cop*.

He had a brilliant career ahead of him in law enforcement. But as his career progressed, his marriage deteriorated.

Bob's wife had been a go-go dancer. He had married her when she was seventeen, and the relationship was not a happy one. One of the major reasons, according to Bob, was that his wife ran up large bills at department stores. She was spending more than he was earning.

That put pressure on Bob to earn extra money. In his spare time, he did everything from washing cars to putting in as much extra duty as he could at the department, working several nights a week with the armed robbery detail.

But the debts always exceeded Bob's ability to repay. Finally, he and his wife were divorced. She was given custody of their young son. "I never missed her," Bob says, "but I missed my boy. I'd do anything in the world for him."

Frowning, Bob declares that when he was arrested in Phoenix his whole life changed.

"All of a sudden, from a *Super Cop* I was a *Super Hunted Criminal*, labeled as the "Catch Me" killer. It was reported on newscasts that I was armed with automatic weapons, had a bulletproof vest, hand grenades and dynamite, that I'd kill my weight in wildcats, and that I'd sooner die than be taken captive. All that stuff wasn't true. I was frightened. I was really scared. That's why I gave myself up."

During the seven months he spent in county jail pending trial, he recalls, "I became an animal. All the inmates knew I'd been a police officer. I was assaulted on several occasions, and had to go to the hospital. I had a very, very bad time adjusting to confinement.

"But I had hope. I was sure I would be exonerated. I had no recollection of commiting any crime."

Nor, says Bob, did he have any recollection of his trial.

"All I know is that one day I was a *Super Cop* and a patriotic Green Beret. The next day the papers made me a super *maniac*, a killer who was just a mad dog, and a karate expert who was going to jump on everybody and destroy people, which wasn't so. I went through a process of losing my memory and identity."

Prison was far worse than county jail for Bob. He spent his first seven months in isolation.

"After that, on my first day out of *The Hole*, I was lying on a bench in the yard, trying to get some sun. Nine inmates assaulted me with a two-by-four.

"One swipe broke my teeth. I had to spit them into my hand. The other blows broke my nose and jaw.

"I went berserk. All the rage, all the reporters who'd heckled me, all the people who had turned against me, all the hostility that I had, all the fear, came out.

"I just went crazy and fought back against the inmates who were attacking me. They relent if you fight back. That was the only law. It was the law of the jungle, of the tooth and claw.

"I managed to break a couple of jaws and some ribs. Again, I became a wild animal. I was fighting for my life.

"Fortunately, I was able to run these cons off. After that, everybody started to respect me as an individual who would not take any hard time from other inmates.

"As a result of my injuries, I had to have plastic surgery, a new set of teeth, and over a hundred stitches in my head."

After serving four years at the state prison, Bob had calmed down. He appeared ripe for rehabilitation, and was transferred to a lightly guarded institution at Belle Glade, Florida. (The institution, however, was surrounded by an alligator-choked moat. The prisoners called the man-eaters their "pets" and named one *Snaggletooth.*)

Not yet a Christian, and still enthralled by the idea that freedom from prison would mean happiness for him, Bob managed to escape, triggering a coast-to-coast manhunt.

Bob escaped from Belle Glade by jumping a fence and swimming the moat. Luckily, he avoided *Snaggletooth* and his ferocious friends. "Another two minutes in that water and those 'gators would have had me," says Bob.

A hue and cry went up following Bob's escape.

"The $64,000 question is what Bob Erler was doing at the Belle Glade facility," said one law enforcement official. "I'm wondering on what basis it was decided to put a man who was serving a prison term for murder in a place like that, which isn't equipped to handle maximum security prisoners."

Captain Sam Martin, a detective on the Hollywood Police Department force, feared revenge. He said he was "a little nervous" about Bob's escape because many of the men who'd helped put him in prison still worked for the department.

Belle Glade Superintendent Philip Shuford didn't think Bob would try to avenge himself. "We had no problems whatsoever with Erler until his escape."

The superintendent's assessment was accurate. Survival, not revenge, was the engine driving Bob Erler.

"I went out through the Everglades," he says. "I swam through bayous, the muck, and the canals, and I got away."

He made it to Mississippi, "where I got involved with organized crime. I got heavily involved with people whom I had met in the state prison and in Belle Glade. I kind of admired them. I felt they were really tough guys.

"I figured maybe my calling was to be a *super criminal* instead of a Super Cop. I didn't really know.

"These people were into every kind of crime. They were professional killers and jewel thieves. They counterfeited money. They transported stolen cars across state lines. They even moonshined whisky.

"I stayed with them for three months. But when one of my friends was found shot to death, it terrified me. I figured maybe this kind of life is too tough, maybe I'm not really a tough guy."

That impression was reinforced when a house in which Bob was hiding was surrounded by the police and the FBI.

"I looked out the window and I saw all those people in uniform and plain clothes. They all had their guns drawn, so my natural assumption was that they were there to arrest me.

"I figured that with my notoriety as the "Catch Me" killer, I'd be gunned down on sight. So I hid in the bedroom closet when they came into the house."

Bob could not only hear the conversation of two officers as they searched the room, "but I could hear one of them breathe; he couldn't have been more than eighteen inches away from me.

"I said to myself, 'I hope he doesn't open the closet door.' I had a *.45* in my hand and I didn't know what would come out of me, the good guy or the bad guy. One side of my mind said, 'Bob, this man is a brother. He's a police officer and you can't hurt him.' The other side of my mind said, 'You've escaped from a ninety-nine-and-a-half-year sentence and you don't want to go back.'

"There was a war going on in my head. I was afraid. I didn't actually know what would happen, so I said a prayer: *Please, God, don't let this officer open the door, please.*"

The policeman failed to open the door because his attention was distracted by the discovery of contraband stashed in a corner.

"Hey, Mike," his buddy yelled, "look here, machine guns, rifles, all kinds of weapons and burglary tools."

The officers confiscated the *cache* and left the room.

"Then," says Bob, "after I was sure they were all gone I came out of the closet, walked into the kitchen and left my gun on the refrigerator. I realized that what I now call the devil made me consider the possibility of killing that police officer. I also realized that I wasn't a killer, nor a professional criminal. I knew that all my frustrations, my hate, the negative feelings I had, and all my animosities, were my problems. The officers were good people, law and order was good, and I was wrong."

Still Bob didn't give himself up. He'd disguised himself by growing a mustache and long hair, so it was fairly easy for him to travel undetected.

He went all over the country. He remembers stopping in Memphis and Chicago and then doubling back to Mississippi, without, however, seeing his friends in crime.

He got a job in a construction gang working as a common laborer, digging ditches. The temperature was twenty-six or twenty-seven degrees above zero. But Bob liked the work and hated to see the job end.

Word got to Bob that because he'd left the gang, there was a contract out on his life. He thus decided to leave Mississippi as soon as he received a gun he'd ordered through the mail, a 3.57 Magnum.

"Coming through the mail they either X-rayed it, or they dropped it at the post office," says Bob. "Somehow they found out it was a weapon and that it was addressed to me."

Bob was unaware when he walked to the general delivery window of the post office in a small town near Jackson, that the place was staked out by sheriff's men, the FBI, and postal inspectors.

When he asked the clerk if there was a package for him, the woman ducked under the counter.

"Boy, did I know something was wrong! I ran outside, got into my car and sped away. When I hit the first intersection, eight police cars converged on me. Some of the deputies were hanging out of the windows with sawed-off shotguns. They shouted at me to pull over."

Bob felt betrayed. He hadn't committed a crime since his escape; therefore the police ought to leave him alone.

"I guess I wasn't thinking logically. The authorities didn't know I hadn't done anything wrong from the time I got out of Belle Glade. I chose to forget that I still had a long, long sentence to serve.

"I felt let down. I just decided that I would either be free or that they would have to kill me."

Bob temporarily eluded the roadblock by swerving sharply through fences and yards.

"I just ran people off the road, and drove at 120 to 125 miles an hour. I lost all the federal officers, but the sheriff had a *souped-up* car with a 454 Chevy engine, and he was faster than I was."

Bob's car was hit forty-five times with shotgun blasts. The windows and back tires were knocked out and bullets were sailing past his head.

"I jumped out of the car and started running into a field. At that point, I didn't care anymore. There was just no meaning in life. I was that lost.

"As I ran, I was nicked by a bullet. Those bullets were cutting the grass, raising hills of dirt around me. It was unbelievable. Shotguns—rifles—pistols.

"Then, when I was seventy-five yards from them, I was hit in the lower back. I was losing blood all over the place. The bullet had gone into one side of my body and come out the other. I thought my hip was shattered. I was hobbling, trying to make it toward a grove of trees. But they had a car and caught up to me."

Bob screamed profanities at the lawmen. He begged them to finish him off.

"Kill me! Please kill me! Just kill me!"

He was quickly handcuffed, and one deputy said, "I *ought* to kill you. I should blow your head off."

"Do it! Do it!"

All of a sudden, according to Bob, the sheriff arrived. A muscular, well-built, large man, he seemed to have a mean look on his face.

"Kill me, sheriff. Come on, just one shot in the head. . . ."

The sheriff stared at Bob, and looked him square in the eyes.
"Nobody's going to kill you," he said. "I love you, and Jesus
Christ loves you."

Bob says, "I couldn't believe the words I was hearing; they
just blew my mind. His name is Bill Middleton, and he's one
of the most beautiful persons in the world."

Bob was patched up in town. While waiting to be sent back
to Florida after six eventful months of freedom, he talked often
with Sheriff Middleton.

"He never pushed Christ on me. He would just mention
occasionally that God has a purpose for everyone's life. He told
me he was a Christian and that I should look into the Scriptures."

After Bob was returned to Florida State Prison, he spent
fourteen months in *The Hole* as punishment for his escape.

"What the heck," he says, "I didn't have anything else to
do, so I thought I might as well study the Bible. Let me find
out what everybody is talking about—all this funny religious
stuff.

"Who is Jesus Christ?

"What is this religious fantasy trip everybody's on?"

Bob not only began reading the Bible, but he also took an
extension course in religion from the University of Florida. His
grade was *A* plus.

Then, like life-giving water trickling through to the roots of
a plant, understanding of God reached Bob.

"I realized that when I was a Green Beret and had a mal-
function on a parachute jump that God fixed it for me. I always
considered that just a lucky break. But it was Jesus Christ
working in my life. I never would accept that. I didn't want to
believe that.

"I realized that when I'd been chased by the police in
Mississippi and shot twice, it was Jesus who saved my life. I
realized that when I was in that closet, on the verge of killing
a policeman, that God would have made me do the right thing.

"I believe to this day that I was saved when I was in that
closet, when the warring factions in my mind were the devil
and Jesus. Praise the Lord, Jesus was mightier than the devil."

With those thoughts in mind, Bob says, "I felt I would be a perfect candidate for Christianity. So I officially became a Christian."

But then, confessed Bob, he was filled with doubts—"I'm a hypocrite because I have doubts, because I don't really believe. This is just an emotional thing."

Thinking it through, Bob decided to put God to a test. He asked himself what was the one thing he wanted most in the world.

"The only thing I really cared about was my son. I hadn't seen him nor my ex-wife for more than seven years. I'd had no letters or communication of any kind. I didn't even know in which state they were living.

"I said a simple little prayer, *Jesus Christ, Lord, God, whatever You call Yourself, if You're real, I want You to let me know my son, because I love him.*"

Two weeks later, Bob was told by a guard that he had two visitors.

"And there was my little boy and my ex-wife. For no reason, they decided after seven years that they wanted to come and visit me. I didn't know what to say. My little boy, Bobby, is just so beautiful, Chaplain, it's incredible.

"I asked him, 'Do you like your dad?'

"And Bobby answered, 'No, I don't like you. I *love* you.'

"Then he gave me a big kiss, and I started crying. And I knew that Jesus Christ was working in my life. I knew Jesus had a plan for me, too."

Shortly thereafter, Bob placed his phone call to me in Dallas and asked me to visit him.

He said he'd killed Merilyn Clark and shot her mother.

"I've been led by God to admit this. If I call myself a Christian, then I am a Christian. There's no borderline. You are either a Christian or you're not. I'm being punished for my crimes, and I should be. God is going to decide how long I'll be in prison, twenty years, thirty years, or the rest of my life. . . .

"I've pulled my appeal out of court. I am no longer appealing through the *court of man.* My appeal is to Jesus Christ. If He wants me in prison, I'm staying in prison. If He wants me out, then I'll be out."

Several publishers and Hollywood producers are interested in a book and film about Bob's life.

"Up to now I turned them all down. But since I've become a practicing Christian I want the book to be written and a movie made."

I asked Bob why.

Because, he said, he's become a believer in the biblical injunction to make restitution.

"There are so many people who go to prison and profit from their crimes. They make all this money from a book and a movie, and the victim of the crime is never compensated. I feel this is wrong. I feel Jesus wants me to do the right thing.

"Mrs. Clark is still alive. She has these large hospital bills and she's suffered terribly because of me.

"I should be made to pay her bills. I should pay all her medical expenses and also give her a sum of money."

Bob says the rest of the money from the rights to his story would be set aside for his son—"since I'm not the father I should be"—and for a fund to start a non-profit organization for the needs of inmates, especially juvenile offenders.

"I don't want people to think that I went to prison, and now want to make a lot of money by publicizing my crimes.

"I don't want to make anything from it. I want to help people. That's the Christian way. I want to show people that, and, hopefully, my example will touch the hearts of other inmates who will compensate the victims of their crimes."

Bob Erler, the "Catch Me" killer who became a living witness for Christ, has no doubt about his future.

"The Bible says to confess your sins. I have confessed my sins to Jesus, and I know I'm going to heaven. My reward will come in heaven. That's the only reward that interests me."

11

Revive Us Again

We praise Thee, O God! for the Son of Thy love,
For Jesus who died, and is now gone above.
Hallelujah! Thine the glory, Hallelujah! Amen.
Hallelujah! Thine the glory, Revive us again.

There is more Christian action in penal institutions today—
soul winning, prayer and Bible study—than in the entire two-
hundred-year history of the American prison system.

And that's as it should be, for the very word *penitentiary*
owes its origin to religion. The Quakers established the belief
in the eighteenth century that if criminals were given religious
instruction and time to reflect, they would become *penitent*
and change.

Nevertheless, for too many years Christian witnesses were
kept out of prisons or discouraged from taking a vibrant, active
daily role in the lives of prisoners.

Finally, all that is changing. The entire prison establish-
ment, from guards to ivory-tower crimininologists, are seeing
a wave of unprecedented revival behind the walls. The *experts*
are confounded. The professional penologists supposedly had
the solutions to rehabilitation and recidivism, and they tried
every conceivable experiment with one noble exception—
Christ.

Now the doors of penitentiaries and jails are swinging wide
open for Christian messengers who have the only pragmatic

answer to what ails the prison system and prisoners.

"Christ is alive and working in this prison and it's unbelievable," declares Bob Erler. "We've had so many conversions to
Christianity, so many sincere people who have found Christ,
that I'm just overwhelmed."

Chaplain Dale Hatfield of the Florida State Prison confirms
Bob's enthusiasm. "Several hundred of the prison's eleven hundred inmates are involved in a spiritual awakening," he says.

> We praise Thee, O God! for Thy spirit of light,
> Who hath shown us our Saviour, and scatter'd our night.
> Hallelujah! Thine the glory, Hallelujah! Amen.
> Hallelujah! Thine the glory, Revive us again.

In order to increase prison revival and thus lessen crime, we
need thousands of additional practicing Christians in the penitentiaries and in law enforcement. We need more chaplains,
more Christian wardens, correctional officers, policemen and
sheriffs. Look at what a Christian sheriff was able to achieve
in the darkest moment of Bob Erler's life.

When we have prison chaplains who are allowed to function,
who have the freedom to spread the gospel, three important
things are accomplished:

First, the growing body of Christian convicts who've
turned from lust, sin, violence and all the evils that are so
prevalent in prisons, to living the Christian life of love, peace
and purity, affect the climate of the institutions. Tensions are
reduced; so is violence. Interpersonal relationships are im-
proved. There is more beneficial communication between
guards and convicts, and between convicts and the highest
levels of the prison administration.

Secondly, chaplains win many prisoners to Christ—and
that's rehabilitation! Living for God speeds the spiritual recov-
ery of prisoners so they can be released at an earlier date into
the free world. Thus years are shaved from their sentences and
millions of dollars are saved by taxpayers.

Thirdly, chaplains greatly reduce recidivism. When these
born-again prisoners go out, they invariably stay out. They

seldom return as a result of committing new crimes.

In one prison I visited not long ago a converted convict, on the verge of parole, told me:

"You know, Chaplain Ray, for years I was just another smart aleck con in the yard. The cons here, myself included, persecuted Christians. We made fun of them. We ridiculed them. We called them 'Jesus freaks.' We called them 'religious kooks.' But they came and they went; they came and they went. I finally realized that there was something different about those convicts who were Christians. When they were released, they didn't come back to prison. It got through to me at last that Christ works."

How *real,* how *lasting,* how *deep* is the swell of prison revival?

Very real. Very lasting. Very deep.

Charles Colson was President Nixon's special counsel, and the "hatchet man" of the White House. Snared in the Watergate scandal, he served seven months in two federal prisons for spreading derogatory information about Daniel Ellsberg.

Colson's conversion, which occurred before he entered prison, was remarkable, illustrating that no man, however powerful, is beyond the reach of Jesus.

While he was incarcerated, Colson became extremely interested in what Christ could accomplish in the lives of other prisoners.

Following his release, he formed a widespread, effective evangelical prison ministry, Fellowship Foundation, which has the approval of the Federal Bureau of Prisons. The work is supported by Colson's speaking engagements and royalties from his bestselling book, *Born Again.*

"Miracles are happening in prisons," he says. "Lives, thousands of them, are being changed on a lasting basis."

Though there aren't enough Christians in the prison mission field, their number is growing. Scores of organizations with thousands of dedicated church members are seeking out prisoners for a life-changing experience with Christ.

Typical of these God-inspired organizations, and one of the

most potent, is Christian Jail Workers of Los Angeles, which, through voluntary donations, supports fifteen full-time prison chaplains and fields a volunteer force of 450 members. Christian Jail Workers reaches men and women in twenty-four institutions. They counsel, encourage the reading of Scripture and hold worship services.

In February 1976 alone, Christian Jail Workers registered 525 definite decisions for Christ and counseled 1,700 other inmates.

Even the grim atmosphere of San Quentin is being charged with the electric word of the Lord. Correctional Officer Thomas Plummer: "I find much encouragement from the recent interest that has been expressed towards faith in Christ. I see a great many inmates carrying their personal Bibles everywhere—not only to chapel services but to meals."

> All glory and praise to the Lamb that was slain,
> Who hath borne all our sins, and hath cleans'd every stain.
> Hallelujah! Thine the glory, Hallelujah! Amen.
> Hallelujah! Thine the glory, Revive us again.

I never enter a prison without leading someone to the Lord, or laying the groundwork for a later conversion. Thomas DeJarnette, an inmate at the Ohio State Prison, found my ministry helpful, and I cherish a poem he wrote expressly for me, entitled "A Tribute to Chaplain Ray":

> There was this Chaplain, his name is Ray,
>   He preached the Gospel every day.
> He spoke to men behind prison walls,
>   And told them that Christ died for all.
> Some of these men are forgotten by friends,
>   They suffer broken hearts on life's last end.
> For they are prisoners for some big crime,
>   And some not guilty, for as much as a dime.
> Now some men are preachers, and some are sent,
>   But this Brother Ray never asked for a cent.

I heard him preach on a radio wall,
  In a prison cell, when I made this fall.
He sent me books and a Bible, too,
  Now I have salvation and this is true.
For when the Master heals a broken heart,
  It's just the beginning, and only a start.
Because I have fought a mighty good fight,
  And I love the Lord with all my might,
And when I die, and go my way,
  I can give my thanks to Chaplain Ray.

In every prison I visit, in every conversation I have about the Lord with a prisoner, I tell him that in my pocket I'm carrying a *pardon* with his name on it. The tired eyes show sparkle, the careworn face displays interest.

My *pardon*, I explain, consists of six steps—the six steps to Jesus:

1. Repentance begins the Christian life. Repentance also continues it. Repentance allows us, as sinners, to make contact, to speak and to commune with God. When a Christian has permitted his fellowship with God to be broken or damaged by the presence of sin in his life, full fellowship can only be restored by confession and repentance.

God has commanded all men, everywhere, to repent.
What is repentance?
It is simply being sufficiently sorry for your sins and turning away from them.
And how do we repent?
Repentance is intellectual, emotional and revolutionary.
First, we change our thinking about sin—no longer condoning, no longer excusing, no longer enjoying it.
Next, we change our thinking about ourselves. We must recognize that our sin is not our brother's or our father's or our mother's or our friend's sin. We must tear the mask from our own sins, no longer calling them inconsequen-

tial, harmless, or mere personality defects or characteristics.

We must see ourselves as sinners. Then as we see God as holy, righteous and just, we respond to His matchless grace and love.

2. You must first seek the kingdom of God and His righteousness. Adoniram Judson was a missionary in Burma for many years, but without a single convert. His church in New York finally wrote him, asking, "What are the prospects for winning men to Christ?"

He answered, "The prospects are as bright as the promises of God."

After reminding himself of that, this pioneer missionary reaped a great harvest of souls in Burma because now he placed God's kingdom first in his life.

If Jesus had not put first things first would He have gone to the Cross? He put our redemption first.

Now He wishes us to organize our lives, to direct them toward great goals and purposes—*His* goals and purposes.

He wants us to be fishers of men—every day, everywhere, every one of us. And those of us who put other things first are missing the joys and glories of knowing God.

Those who put Him first find each day an exhilarating quest. They are the ones of whom someone has said, "A Christian is a person who does ordinary things in an extraordinary way."

3. Let your light shine before men so that you may glorify God. Exodus 34:35 tells us that Moses, after God spoke with him, did not realize that his face was shining.

The faces of all Christians, when they listen to God, shine, though they seldom realize it. Such holy and personal communion leaves them oblivious to self.

One Christian responded to those who criticize the Bible: "They may tear the volume to shreds, but they can never rub off the light of God from the faces of His people!"

What is this outer glow?

It is the reflection of inner fires caused by the excitement of God. It means that God's people are living in the light of the grandest, most supreme experience that life offers.

When we live in the shadow of our lowest, darkest, meanest hours we totally fail to glorify God.

The Christ-glorifying life is one that is lived in the present, with a daily, hourly relationship to God. There is no looking back with guilt and grief, nor even longing for tomorrow, but a glowing awareness of God—*NOW!*

4. The good fight of faith must be fought.

There has never been any work accomplished for God without opposition. A great many people are afraid of conflict. They run for cover. But if there is to be any real, lasting work done for the Lord, Satan will see to it that there will be a battle.

The Bible abounds with examples of men whose faith conquered all—from Abraham to the Disciples.

To possess faith means that conflict will present itself, but with belief in God's promises we meet the battles with confidence and courage.

5. Even as you are forgiven, you must forgive. Forgiveness is what happened on the cruel Cross of Calvary. Even though His Son suffered terribly, God forgave us. His forgiveness changed despair to hope, death to life.

Because He forgave, we too must learn to forgive.

St. Francis said, "It is in pardoning that we are pardoned."

Our forgiveness of others does not earn our forgiveness from

God, but it makes it possible for God's freely given forgiveness to be showered on us.

6. Glorify God in body and spirit.

This is the magnificent goal of the Christian, but how is such
a high calling achieved?
With our bodies we express ourselves—indifference or concern, hate or love, fear or faith. Christ is judged by those
who are His. The believer must manifest Christ, show
Christ to the world. Jesus said in Acts 1:8, ". . . ye shall
be witnesses unto me. . . ."
A witness is one who tells something he knows. But do we
tell our friends, do we tell everyone we meet, about the
glory of the resurrected Christ?
Only through the ascended Christ can we witness at all. God
wants our entire life to be a witness, a testimony.
To glorify God in body and spirit must remain the goal of
the Christian. He can hardly do less, when Jesus did so
much.

After I've explained Christ's pardon, I ask the prisoner to
pray with me:

*Heavenly Father, I know that I am a sinner and I ask for Your
mercy. I believe Christ died for my sins. I repent of my sins and
I ask Your forgiveness. I am willing to turn from my sins and
my old way of life and to live for You. I now invite Jesus Christ
to come into my heart as my personal Savior. I will follow and
obey Christ, by Your grace, making Him the Lord of my life,
from this day forward.*

I also tell the prisoner that if he has prayed truly and sincerely he is now a child of God. How can he be sure? Because
the Bible tells him.
John 11:25–26: ". . . I am the resurrection, and the life:
he that believeth in me, though he were dead, yet shall he

live: And whosoever liveth and believeth in me shall never die. . . ."

And John 1:12: "But as many as received him, to them gave he power to become the sons of God, even to them that believeth on his name."

> Revive us again; fill each heart with Thy love;
> May each soul be rekindled with fire from above.
> Hallelujah! Thine the glory, Hallelujah! Amen.
> Hallelujah! Thine the glory, Revive us again.

I've been called America's "Cellblock Chaplain," a title that gives me a great deal of satisfaction. The title is also a challenge: Until all our penitentiaries are empty because every soul behind bars has been won for Christ, my work and the work of others won't be finished.

Hallelujah! Thine the glory, Hallelujah! Amen.

Let's also hear a loud amen for what has already been accomplished in moving prisoners from crime to Christ.

And somebody say amen for the miracles in the lives of Susan Atkins and Tex Watson.

An amen, too, for *The Meanest Man in Texas*, Clyde Thompson.

Another amen for Floyd Hamilton, onetime *Public Enemy Number 1*.

Let's hear an amen for Murf the Surf, Gene Neill and Bob Erler.

And for His blessings and forgiveness and deliverance and everlasting life, by all means someone shout *Amen* for Jesus.

Amen!